D0125731

come an immediate reality instead of an ultimate goal. This was the dire emergency that caused the spectacular creation of the State of Israel.

II

Zionism represents the modern organized effort in the historical aspirations of the Jewish people to reconstitute itself partly or wholly as a political, economic, religious and cultural entity in its ancient homeland. Its program is all-encompassing, rooted in the experience of Jews, inspired by their traditions and fused by the cataclysmic events of the twentieth century. The Zionist solution to the Jewish problem takes in land, language, religion, culture, society and personality. Theory is combined with practice in promoting a revolt against the abnormal existence of a people in exile, with its concomitant limitations and deterrents to the welfare of the group and the fulfillment of the individual. The aforementioned factors, instrumental in the emerging supremacy of the Zionist formula, have given rise to fundamental values spelling out the meaning of Zionism.

What are the ideological components basic to Israel society, championed by its pioneers and intellectual leaders, though not always shared by the public at large? The history and literature of the modern Israel experience emphasize six sancta which make up the Zionist credo and constitute the spiritual substructure upon which the new State was founded. These command the loyalty of the secular community to no less a degree, if not greater, than that of the religious.

(a) Zionism is fundamentally inseparable from the Messianic dream of redemption with its *universalistic* as well as particularistic ramifications. Though focused on one people, it sweeps the panorama of mankind. Judaism, from its inception, has projected into the future the inevitability of universal redemption, peace and brotherhood brought about by the work of man and the grace of God. Yet the ultimate triumph of justice and freedom for all would not be complete without the restoration of the people of Israel to its land, and the spiritual rejuvenation of Zion. The Jewish Messiah, destined to appear, will find a leading spiritual role for Israel in the new scheme of things in the World to Come.

Stripped of its theological embellishment, the messianic yearning has not left untouched even the secular Jew. Justice to the Jewish people requires recognition of its historic association with the Holy Land and a vindication of the unswerving faith in its restoration. This is essential in the blueprint of the New World. Ancillary to this striving is the cherished hope for "a new light to shine upon Zion," illuminating the path of mankind once again. Messianic Zionism of this dimension has been characteristic of rabbis, mystics and legalists throughout the ages. It pervades the writings of modern secularists as well.

The forerunners of Zionism in the 19th century affirmed this proposition. Among them were the rabbis Zvi Kalisher and Judah Alkalai, who represented the Ashkenazi and Sfardi traditions respectively. Striking a similar note was the socialist-intellectual and compatriot of Marx, Moses Hess who wrote in German. Kalisher, Alkalai and Hess, individually, formulated their views in the decades of the mid-century, disseminating their ideas through the written and spoken word.

(b) An integral aspect of this messianic era is the concept of "*Ingathering of Exiles*," a phrase in vogue even in the contemporary terminology of official pronouncements. The dispersion of Jewry throughout the globe is to be remedied by the return of large numbers to Israel. The age of the Messiah will usher in the necessary course of events. One dramatic example of the power of this faith is the speed by which the entire Jewish community of Yemen, over 50,000 souls, was transported to Israel immediately after the founding of the State.[2] To this, as well as to other communities, the State of Israel spelled out the miracle of redemption and the oportunity to return after two thousand years of exile.

The objective of the Ingathering is both to amass numerical strength and to gather and sustain the erstwhile scattered remnants of the prolonged dispersion. In the five year period following independence, immigrants came to Israel out of six continents from thirty-four officially recorded countries of origin.[3] What makes this so remarkable is the fact that these thirty-four sources of emigration were of diverse tongues and cultures, yet the migratory contingents were all of the same religious faith and members of a people which numbers less than thirteen million throughout the world.

The promise of redemption was originally interpreted as divine intervention. It was re-defined by Zionism in terms of historical development and human initiative, directed toward the companion goals of political independence in Palestine and the return of the scattered brethren—in the words of the traditional prayer book—"from the four corners of the earth". Subsequently, this was to lead to a higher status for Jews abroad, elevating them from a persecuted and helpless minority to an accepted equal, the stigma of homelessness to be replaced by the banner of national sovereignty, their collective inferiority complex to be substituted by self-respect leading to recognition and acceptance as peers.

The rush of events substantially vindicated the faith and

the program of Zionism. Thus a state destroyed in 70 and resurrected in 1948, eighteen hundred and seventy eight years after its demise, seen in the perspective of all that has transpired, can hardly be overestimated in its impact on the formation of the national character. The faith, challenges and promises in messianic dimensions continue to inspire the thought and acts of Israel leaders, infiltrating the program of the schools, and charging both literature and the arts.

(c) A third Zionist goal, interwoven with the first two, is the *socio-economic*. Along with the restoration of the homeland and the reconstitution of the people, there follows the remodeling of its economic structure. Various methods and degrees of change were propounded by differing schools of thought ranging from radical social upheaval to less revolutionary programs. The prophetic ideal of Social Justice, combined with adaptations of Marxism, captured the allegiance of the Palestinian pioneer at the beginning of the twentieth century. He rebelled against the humiliations and frustrations imposed upon the Jew by a hostile world. He protested against the prevailing economic patterns of Jewish society. He also tried to escape the injustice of capitalistic exploitation and the glaring inequalities of its economy.

The neo-Marxist reinterpretations of Austrian theoreticians were applied to the Jewish scene. In the early part of this century Ber Borochov saw the opportunity for a "productive" proletariat in Palestine to replace the "unproductive" and rootless *Luftmensch* of the Russian Jewish communities and the *petite bourgeoisie* of westernized Jewry. Nachman Syrkin, who took issue with dogmatic Marxist doctrine, further related the Jewish problem to a reconstituted classless system in Palestine, based on the teachings of the prophets and the theories of socialism, the latter to be dissociated from its materialistic connotations and understood in its idealistic aspirations.

A. D. Gordon preached and practiced the message of "personal realization" in a return to nature and the soil, and the spiritual rehabilitation of the individual through the salutary effects of physical labor. A youthful, embittered but yet enthusiastic generation dedicated itself to this task, adopting the faith and practice of the "religion of labor", as Gordon's philosophy was termed. Thousands of youthful idealists streamed from the shattered hopes of the Old World to the beckoning shores of the Promised Land. They mastered Israel's environment with its rocky terrain, infested swamps, hostile inhabitants and inhospitable climate. Initiative and self-sacrifice finally brought about the successful colonization of a neglected land, the establishment of a model society through hundreds of collective villages (*Kibbutzim*), and the rise of organized labor as the most positive and powerful social and spiritual force in Israel today.

It is obvious that this economic philosophy in its entirety cannot be accepted by all segments of Israel society. By and large, the predominantly socialist-oriented pioneer elements, however, in their various political shadings of allegedly distinct demarcations, (ranging from the militant atheistic to the Orthodox religious) have subscribed to these theories. The basic proposition, the revamping of the economic system of European Jewry, was universally affirmed by all schools of Zionist thought, including the "capitalist sector." They recognized the need for a transfer from commercial and clerical pursuits to industry and agriculture, the introduction of necessary controls of a planned economy and the indispensable prerequisite of national ownership of land to facilitate colonization. To achieve this purpose, vocational training institutions in

Palestine sprang up under the auspices of French, German and Russian Jewish agencies. Agricultural training farms (*hachsharot*) to prepare for Palestine, existed for decades in Europe and America. The Jewish National Fund, established in 1901 by the World Zionist Congress for the purchase of land in Palestine, began to make land available for agricultural purposes and to a lesser extent for educational and industrial enterprise, subject to a specific code of operation, "rented" to its occupants for a token fee.

The exigencies of Jewish life have escalated normal development to what may appear to be artificial and lofty heights. Charging an ordinary economic process with idealistic and religious meaning may seem far-fetched. Notice must be taken, however, of the struggle for Jewish survival in the era which came to a close after the first World War. There were historical factors which compelled Jews to concentrate in certain occupations. Prohibitions upon land ownership by Jews were generally in effect throughout Europe. In Russia, the most fertile areas were even outside the official "Pale of Settlement" to which Jews were restricted. Commercial enterprises required fluid assets and depended upon mental acumen rather than physical resources—a necessary condition for self-preservation in the frequent banishments throughout the centuries. It was natural, therefore, that the main occupational activities associated with abnormal existence in the diaspora should be relegated to an inferior position by the Zionist ideal. Beyond this negative consideration there was also the urgent need for farming, heavy industry and skilled labor, all of which were vitally essential to the establishment of firm foundations for a self-sufficient Jewish society in Palestine.

It is in this area, the socio-economic, that the message of Zionism sounded the universal note in its national theme. Espousing world socialism, a classless society, peace among nations and harmony within them, the Zionist pioneers undertook to lead by example. And the experiment succeeded.

It is amazing, though seldom recognized, that the voluntary communistic, agricultural colonies in Israel are probably the only Utopia-inspired experiments in the world which have not failed. In Israel they have flourished since their inception, more than fifty years ago. Today they are numbered in the hundreds. Yet similar American and English ventures of the nineteenth century had to be abandoned, and Russian collectives have never developed into anything more than camps for forced labor.[4]

(d) The *psychological* goal of the Zionist idea, previously referred to, needs further clarification. It is the thesis of Zionism that the personality of the Jew has been scarred and marred by long exile. A victim of circumstances beyond his control, his physical and psychological security constantly threatened, he has become abnormal, i.e. maladjusted both inwardly and outwardly. A balanced mental and emotional pattern of behavior, inner harmony and outer adjustment, may be restored by a changed environment in Israel. The sick soul of the Jew can recuperate and his shattered human dignity can be repaired in the pure and healthful atmosphere of Israel.

These advantages will not accrue spontaneously, nor as the result of passive inaction. No less than a total revolution must take place before a metamorphosis of personality results. Specifically, it will come about in the presence of three conditions. The first of these is a change in the mode of living from the uncertainties and speculative nature of commercial enterprise to the solid stance of physical labor. The second is a change of locale from an urban to a rural setting. The third is a change of attitude toward active self-defense in face of physical attack instead of non-resistance and a scurry to supposed safety.

The first concept, the economic reorientation, has already been discussed from the viewpoint of national urgency. Its intellectual premises will be elaborated upon in the chapters on the socialist theoreticians. The psychological dimension, however, merits immediate scrutiny.

The "grandfather" of modern Yiddish and Hebrew literature, Mendele Mocher Sforim reflected the *Haskala** thesis, that the economic imbalances have caused mental and moral aberrations. The daily uncertainties, flounderings and fumblings, speculations and machinations in the pursuit of the meagre profits eked out for a subsistence on bare necessities, had created habits of thought and social relationships which were often furtive, irregular and unhealthy. Occupational training in productive and skilled labor for employment, because it entailed physical exercise, daily routine, the assurance—or at least the anticipation of—regular income and established patterns, is destined to be of considerable therapeutic value psychologically and emotionally.

The second condition, the return to nature, places a premium upon agriculture in the gamut of gainful occupations. The cramped, shabby quarters of East European Jewish communities ruled out any contact with nature. Bialik, the Hebrew poet of national revival, dramatically depicts how merely pausing to observe the natural wonders of the seasons was regarded as sinful idleness that detracted from the study of the Holy Law.[5] On the other hand, the Bible abounds in idyllic rural description. The Israel landscape offers a tangible tie-in with the spiritually gigantic figures of the Bible, associated with particular locations. The life of a farmer cultivating the soil of the Holy Land is fraught with opportunities for meditation, inspiration

* The Jewish Enlightenment.

and aesthetic experience, all of which are elevating and enriching. Just as Thoreau in New England and Tolstoy in Russia sought to escape the tumult and confusion of urban concentration, the Israel pioneer looked for peace and serenity in the bosom of nature. The devoted proponents of this idea frequently veered far in this direction in the Zionist youth movements which came under their influence, to the point of stressing agricultural pioneering as the only contribution toward the upbuilding of the Jewish Homeland. Such over-emphasis is understandable in the light of the needed ruralization of urban masses and the spiritual opportunity for individual rehabilitation unfolded by the Zionist promise.

The third area of operation, self-defense, is affirmed both as a physical necessity and psychological requirement. Age-old persecution has conditioned the Jew to regard retreat and escape as the only recourses open to him in the face of physical aggression. A defenseless minority without arms at its disposal may find this the only strategy open to it against the overwhelming odds of numerical and military superiority. But a people subject to frequent mob rioting will only invite more attacks by cowardly inaction and flight. The pogroms of Eastern Europe, which erupted when ignorant peasants were incited against Jews by Church and government authorities, inflicted heavy losses on Jewish life, property and honor. The old community of Palestine, as well as the first settlers, were ready targets for Arab violence and conspiracy. The Zionist call for courage and self-defense against attacks opened a new chapter in interfaith relations. Repeated pitched battles discouraged outbreaks and quelled the excited passions of gentile mobs. In Palestine, such tactics took the Arabs by surprise and gained respect for the Zionist pioneers who immediately and effectively had risen to the defense of a threatened community. The Hebrew term for defense, *Hagana,* was added to the sancta of modern Jewish vocabulary.

What is particularly significant in the context of the present analysis is the psychological effect of this change. It brought self-confidence, pride and dignity to Jews hitherto ashamed of their own cowardice. It fostered a new self-image of the Jew, encouraging him to hold his head up and keep his spirits high as he transformed situations of former humiliation to opportunities for self-assuring and reinforcing experience.

The Israel experiment has fashioned a new Jewish type without the conflicts and complexes of the *galut* (exile) personality. A justified sense of achievement has replaced a feeling of inadequacy. Self-acceptance is substituted for the pangs of rejection by others and hate of oneself, so often characteristic of many assimilated Jewish intellectuals including those of prominence. To be at peace with oneself is to disperse tensions and neuroses. Though a sense of equality may dissipate the Chosen People mystique, it will also cancel it as the rationale for passive acceptance of an inferior status. The ability to work hard and well, till the soil and fight bravely in its defense, has bolstered the Jewish ego. The psychological revolution, brought in the wake of the Zionist ideal, has left its impact upon the Jewish personality outside of Israel's borders as well as within them. Shmarya Levin, foremost Zionist orator and propagandist of the past generation, succinctly summarized the Zionist program as dedicated "not only to take the Jew out of a *galut,* but also to take the *galut* out of the Jew." In the words of a contemporary interpreter of the Zionist idea:

> Zionism . . . rather means facing the cold excruciating fact that the restoration of the land to the people is the painfully slow process of the people returning to the land, of individual Jews shouldering the task of returning as individuals, each settling in the land himself, each undergoing the metamorphosis of the returning exile.[6]

(e) Zionism calls for national revival of *cultural* creativity. This applies to language, literature, theater, art and music. To ignore one's own tradition and adopt that of another, to the exclusion of the former, is assimilation. In the realm of religious faith it becomes conversion. Assimilation and conversion, reached by the same process, differ only in degree. They were the looming fate of emancipated Jewry before Zionism appeared on the scene. The awakening of national consciousness expressed itself in a growing attachment to the cultural traditions by the creative continuity of Hebrew letters. Around 1880 J. L. Gordon, poet of the *Haskala*, thought of himself as "the last of the singers of Zion." Two decades later a vibrant dynamic literature again flourished. What made the difference was the Zionist movement.

Since a culture is revealed in a language, Jews faced an added difficulty beyond that of other ethnic minority groups. European Jewry created its own language, Yiddish, building upon medieval German, Hebrew and Slavic components. It developed from a jargon to a rich idiom of expression comparable to other European tongues. Simultaneous to the *Haskala* literature in Hebrew, a cultural heritage of folklore, poetry, prose, drama and journalism was building up in the Yiddish vernacular. At first the masters wrote in both languages; later writers adopted one or the other medium.

Zionism had to choose between a spoken language and the holy tongue, relegated since ancient times to the spiritual. European Jewry was the senior partner in the restoration of the homeland, with little competition or cooperation from Asian and African communities which had not kept pace with cultural advancement. Yet the far-flung tribes of Jewry would be united only through Hebrew. The resurrection of the supposedly "dead" language is an epic tale in itself, presented more fully elsewhere in this book. Zionism became identified with Hebrew in Palestine, but it could not ignore the magnetism of Yiddish in the diaspora as an authentic indigenous Jewish product, a rich treasure expressive of the Jewish spirit, which united European Jews in their dispersion throughout the Americas, Australia and Africa.

In contemporary America, literature may not be a major factor in molding the national character. It generally reflects forces and issues but does not generate the momentum or the direction of their impact. Not so in modern Jewish history. The tremendously important role of Hebrew literature (and to a lesser degree, Yiddish literature) in the Zionist renaissance, cannot be overstressed. The essays of Ahad Ha'am, in their exposition of Zionist theory, were awaited eagerly as they appeared in the periodicals and passed from hand to hand, serving as topics for heated discussion in hundreds of communities throughout Poland, Lithuania and neighboring lands. The poems of Bialik inspired young men to organize illegal self-defense units against peasant mobs. The lyrics of even a second rate minstrel such as M. M. Dolitzki or N. Z. Imber, author of the Zionist anthem *Hatikva*, stirred the souls of tens of thousands and helped to bring many of them to Israel. The short stories of the great writer, Peretz, evoked yearnings and strivings for a finer and better life.

Jewish writing does not fall into the same category as the American dichotomy of newspaper and book. The daily, weekly and monthly periodicals were the organs of expression for the poets, essayists, novelists and dramatists of Hebrew literature. To date, the American Yiddish daily press is the medium for artistic expression which, in its English counterpart, is usually found in philosophical or literary journals, or in special supplements.

For Hebrew literature to emerge as the driving force in

the national resurgence, it had to be released from its religious moorings. It had to begin to depict life in all of its phases, to reflect the inner world of the individual, cope with social, economic, intellectual and emotional problems and experiment with adopting and adapting European literary forms in style, motif, plot and craftsmanship. These elements account for the extension of its scope beyond the borders of aesthetic expression. Modern Hebrew literature, secular as it is, has enjoyed an influence commensurate with the religious books treasured throughout the ages without being either didactic or programmatic. Nevertheless, its standards and values remained under constant scrutiny, resulting in controversies on Europeanism versus Jewishness, aesthetics versus ethics, nationalism versus universalism, and related issues. Poets, novelists, essayists and dramatists had their own coteries of disciples both within and outside of sophisticated circles.

A historian of modern Hebrew literature, Professor Simon Halkin of the Hebrew University, summarizes the role of Hebrew literature in Jewish life and thought:

> From its halting beginnings in the eighteenth century to its latest full-throated utterances in Palestine, Hebrew literature has been intimately connected with all the vital manifestations of Jewish group living, furthering some of them passionately, but often even violently challenging some and bitterly condemning others. More significant still, it has always pioneered among those forces that have impelled and channeled the Jewish group will, calling the group to new forms of living, setting up new standards, anticipating social ideals long before they crystallized into organized movements, creeds and parties.[7]

Much of what has been said about literature applies equally to the press, the theatre and the arts as they were conceived in Europe and transplanted and grafted in Palestine, where they blossomed forth into the reborn Hebrew culture of the Jewish people, with Israel as its spiritual center. The architects of the new Hebraism had planned for it to engage the interests and loyalties of Jews everywhere, prompting and prodding them to partake of a second culture supplementary to that of their country of residence. An international Jewish agency, the *Brit Ivrit Olamit* ("World Hebrew Union") is dedicated to this purpose.[8]

(f) Many Zionists looked forward to a *religious* revival in the Holy Land. The Orthodox wing of the Zionist movement has focused attention upon Israel as the only opportunity for a life compatible with the precepts of the Jewish faith. The Jewish code of civil law, only partially adhered to until the nineteenth century, as against the ritual code which remained largely in effect throughout, became inoperative when Jewish groups relinquished collective ghetto autonomy for personal emancipation, thereby paving the way for a degree of social integration and civil rights for individuals. The social legislation in the Jewish religious code would again be implemented only in an independent state under a Jewish government where Jews make up the majority of the population. The ritual practices, such as Sabbath observance and dietary laws, are retained with little inconvenience in a predominantly Jewish environment. The integration of secular and religious education, without bifurcation into two languages, is possible only in Israel. Furthermore, the ancient Jewish code contains a body of laws applicable only to the Holy Land. The spiritually rewarding opportunity in fulfilling all of the commandments is limited to those who reside in Israel. Judaism could flourish unhampered and regain its pristine glory on the sacred soil.

Religious Zionists have conducted a battle on two fronts

in defense of their position. On the one hand, conservative authoritarian elements still insisted upon waiting for the Messiah to bring them back to Israel, and regarded human initiative in that direction as atheistic violations. On the other side were the articulate secularist elements who, in their enthusiasm to break with minority status outside of Palestine, were eager to reject the religious tradition in its entirety. Among Orthodox Jews, the course of events has tilted the scale in favor of Religious Zionism on the theological issue. In addition, there is a growing appreciation in Israel today of the unique opportunity, and a deeply felt need for a religious revival of unprecedented scope possible only in a Jewish State. Rabbi Abraham Kuk, Chief Rabbi of Palestine, was the inspired exponent of this view.

It is worth noting that American Jewish theological seminaries are presently encouraging resident study in Israel prior to ordination. Strangely enough, the most liberal wing—Reform Judaism—originally anti-Zionist, has taken the lead in this venture. The religious message of Zionism for Israel and Jews abroad is being appreciated to an increasing degree, as the political and economic problems approach satisfactory solution.

III

The ideological and historical foundations of Zionism were well formulated in the preamble to the Declaration of Independence which brought the Jewish State into being on May 15, 1948:

> The Land of Israel was the birthplace of the Jewish people. Here their spiritual, religious and national identity was formed. Here they achieved independence and created a culture of national and universal significance. Here they wrote and gave the Bible to the world. . .

Exiled from Palestine, the Jewish people remained faithful to it in all countries of their dispersion, never ceasing to pray and hope for their return and the restoration of their national freedom. . . .

It is, moreover, the self-evident right of the Jewish people to be a nation, like all other nations, in its own sovereign State. . . .[9]

The Zionist Movement

I

Zionism is the political movement which fathered the State of Israel. It is the modern expression of a two thousand year yearning which nurtured the Jewish spirit throughout the ages. Based on the ancient reality of an independent Jewish State, the memory and the dream were kept alive in faith, ritual, literature and folkways, reinforced by nineteen centuries of homelessness and dispersion. Zionism emerged as a mass force and program of action at the end of the nineteenth century. Within fifty years of its inauguration, the ideal of Jewish statehood was transformed into a fact. No adequate understanding of Israeli society is possible without an awareness of the Zionist movement. Its basic tenets make up the spiritual foundations of life in Israel. The events and personalities of Zionism have been the decisive influences on Israel's destiny.

Prior to 1914, over half the Jews of the world lived in the Russian and Austrian Empires. It was in these areas, among the compact Jewish masses, that a dynamic religious civilization flourished; and it was in this geographic location that new ideas and leaders left their imprint on all of Jewry, Israel and America included.

The nineteenth century found East European Jewry still in the mental climate of the Middle Ages when religion had pervaded all communal, individual, social and intellectual pursuits. Enlightenment came late to European Jewry, for scientific progress and intellectual freedom in European society were accompanied by religious bigotry toward and oppression of the Jewish minority. Catholic universalism had often tolerated Jewish non-conformity. Both Protestant nationalism and Protestant enlightenment were infuriated with persistent Jewish differentness.[10] Economic discrimination, political repression, social isolation and religious persecution kept the Jews of the Dark Ages removed from the illuminating and beneficent effects of the dawn of the new era.

The *Haskala* movement, as Jewish Enlightenment became known in Hebrew, began at the end of the eighteenth century. Moses Mendelssohn, (1729-1786) a scholarly German Jew who became a noted philosopher, was responsible for opening the gates of the ghetto to the culture of Europe. Inspired by his teachings and example, thousands of young men in the towns and villages of Eastern and Central Europe engaged in the study of languages, arts and sciences in a clandestine manner, for this was proscribed by religious authorities. The exponents of the new movement believed that their co-religionists' lack of secular learning stood in the way of their acquiring full citizenship rights and equality of opportunity. The solution to all evils was to be found in a new education that would bring the sciences, the arts, languages and philosophy to the ghetto. The *Haskala* movement, which represented an ever-growing force in Jewish life, in essence was suggesting a new school curriculum as the panacea for all political and economic ills. The overture would be made by the Jewish community and the nations of the world would respond with magnanimity.

The platform upon which Jews were to rise in this brave new world was comparatively easy to construct: a liberal education, a European mode of dress and a gradual shifting to productive labor—particularly farming. Believing in the dawn of a new age, the men of *Haskala* naively felt that once the Jews ate from the modern Tree of Knowledge, the doors to the good life would be thrown open to them.

The products of *Haskala* were diversified. In Germany, the *Haskala* brought religious reform and conversion to Christianity. (Mendelssohn's own grandson, the composer Felix, defected from Judaism.) In Austria and Russia, a secular literature arose in Hebrew, and later in Yiddish. The study of the Bible which, except for the Pentateuch, had long been abandoned for the pursuit of the religious jurisprudence of the Talmud and Codes, was reintroduced; Hebrew grammar and language enjoyed a revival. Mendelssohn's disciple, Naftali Herz Wessely (1725-1805), a poet and pamphleteer for secular education among Austrian Jews, has been regarded by some as the father of modern Hebrew letters.[11] Mendele Mocher Sforim (1835-1917), "grandfather" of modern Yiddish literature, satirized the unwholesome and unaesthetic nature of Jewish life, its socio-economic structure and stifling intellectual atmosphere. The leading Hebrew poet of the times, J. L. Gordon (1830-92), sang of the virtues of *Haskala* and deplored the maze of ritual legalism interfering with individual freedom and happiness. A host of other writers joined in the praise of modernism. Hebrew literature became primarily didactic and moralistic, though it was released from its religious mold and flourished in its adopted secularistic freedom. In the meantime, the Russian government had given some indication that the process of enlightenment would bring reward, and the disciples of the movement were thereby bolstered in their zeal.

The seeming panacea soon proved to be a mirage. There came the pogroms of 1881, engineered by the Czarist regime. In the ashes of destroyed Jewish communities lay the extinguished hopes and promises of the *Haskala.* This was echoed in the call of Gordon, "king of the poets:" "Back to your tents, O Israel!" Europe had disappointed them. The Jewish intelligentsia suddenly awoke to the realization that the Jewish problem would not be solved by benevolence from without, but by concerted initiative from within. Pinsker published his epoch-making pamphlet —a classic of Zionism—*Auto-Emancipation,* focusing attention upon Jewish homelessness and pointing to the need for a separate territory as the end to the road of persecution traversed for nearly two thousand years. The *Hibbat Zion* ("Love of Zion") movement was launched, and the first group of young volunteers (*Bilu*) set out for Palestine as the vanguard of masses destined to return and rebuild the ancient homeland. Hebrew and Yiddish writers reversed their invidious praise and criticism, to favor their own people. Hundreds of thousands of Jews streamed to America and the Argentine; a rivulet trickled on to Palestine.

II

Forerunners of the Zionist movement already appeared in the first half of the nineteenth century. Benjamin Disraeli, born a Jew but converted in childhood to Christianity, published a novel, *Tancred,* on the theme of Israel's return to Zion. The English novelist, George Eliot, depicted the ideal Jew restored to his homeland in *Daniel Deronda.* An American statesman of the Jewish faith, Mordecai Manuel Noah, sought to found a Jewish territory as "an asylum temporary and provisionary . . . under the protection of the American Constitution without relinquishing hope of eventually regaining possession of their ancient homeland."[12] In Prussia, Rabbi Zvi Kalisher (d. 1874) preached the message of return and urged the adoption of practical measures in the settlement of the Holy Land. Palestine-born Rabbi Judah Alkalai (d. 1869), occupying a pulpit in Serbia, suggested a political organization representative of European Jewry to negotiate with the Great Powers and Turkey. David Gordon, editor of the all-important Hebrew periodical *Hamagid,* opened the pages of this *Haskala* organ to the exponents of the new idea and joined their ranks in propagating Zionism.

A romantic setting for the precursors of Zionism was provided by the middle of the century in the works of Abraham Mapu (1808-67). This learned Lithuanian Jew, of scholarly stock, fired the imagination of generations of young people by his dramatic and romantic novels of Judean life in the days of the First Temple. Far removed from Palestine in space and time, climate and environment, he yet captured the fragrance of Judean hills and valleys, and revived the Biblical landscape in his poetic and imaginative re-enactment of a historic setting. Into the crowded, dreary, impoverished villages of the Russian Pale he brought the romance and radiance of a glorious past, and increased the passion for immediate redemption.[13]

These spokesmen came from the ranks of traditional Jewry to whom they directed their message. In 1862 a distant voice was heard when Moses Hess, socialist philosopher and assimilated intellectual of Western Europe, appeared with his German book *Rome and Jerusalem,* a repudiation of assimilationist policies and an exposé of the failure of emancipation, calling for the establishment of a Jewish homeland in Palestine. Seven years later, Peretz Smolenskin, leading Hebrew novelist and essayist, founded in Vienna the monthly *Hashahar* ("The Dawn") dedicated to the revival of Hebrew as the literary medium of Israel's national spirit. Smolenskin preached national cultural rejuvenation and exerted profound influence on the younger generation. Joining other writers of the age, he sensed the utter bankruptcy of *Haskala,* which, in the process of bringing Western enlightenment, alienated the Jew from his people and led to the disappearance of the Jewish identity.

The aforementioned events of 1881 brought to the foreground latent tendencies as well as personalities shocked into a re-appraisal of previously held positions on Jewish nationalism. In addition to the pioneer spirits who plowed the rough terrain of Jewish consciousness and planted the first seeds of Zionism, outside factors influenced the rise of Zionism. There were nationalistic stirrings in South Eastern Europe, uprising of minorities against Turkish domination, giving birth to new states. The upsurge of national consciousness, the desire for independence and the emphasis on ethnic culture generated parallel sentiments among Jews. Thus, when the crisis broke, the weather was not inclement for the new ideas to sprout.

The first pioneers, known as *Bilu,* (a Hebrew acrostic of the verse "O house of Jacob, come ye and let us go," Isaiah 2:5) some twenty of them, arrived in Palestine in 1882, a few years after the founding by local residents of the first agricultural settlement, Petach Tikva. The arrivals were distinguishable from the native Jews in that: (a) they were young students who came to live, whereas those who had preceded them were the older people who had come to the Holy Land to die; (b) they were European educated, conscious of their mission, inspired with zeal to engage in productive labor—essentially agriculture—while the indigenous population was fanatically pious and supported by the traditional system of charitable collections from abroad. Before leaving Russia, the *Bilu* issued a proclamation as significant in content for the understanding of Zionism as it was naive in form:

What we want:

1. A home in our country. It was given to us by the mercy of God; it is ours as registered in the archives of history.
2. To beg of the Sultan, and if it be impossible to obtain this, to beg that at least we may be allowed to possess it as a state within a larger state; the internal administration to be ours, to have our civil and political rights, to act with the Turkish Empire only in foreign affairs, so as to help our brother Ishmael in his time of need.

We hope that the interests of our glorious nation will arouse our national spirit in rich and powerful men, and that everyone, rich and poor, will give his best labors to the holy cause.[14]

The fact that subsequently, university students of liberal arts proved miserable failures as farmers in a strange land is relatively insignificant. Their historic importance lies in the fact that they ignited the spark that lit the flame for the torchbearers who followed and succeeded.

Chronologically, the *Bilu* were not the first. Twelve years earlier, in 1870, the agricultural school, Mikveh Israel, was founded—the first outpost of modern Jewish colonization in Palestine. The inspiration of Charles Netter, (a leader of the Alliance Israélite Universelle, the French

Jewish agency which pioneered in the promotion and defense of Jewish rights throughout the world) the school exists to the present day as an experimental and training station. But for a number of years it remained an isolated endeavor with little effect on the course of events. The *Bilu* adventure, in contrast, though insignificant in practical achievements, launched a new era. Other colonies followed in the eighties and nineties, while the Zionist societies in Russia were engaged in the two-fold task of supporting the settlers abroad and propagating Zionism at home. The first task was performed primarily with the aid of the Paris baron, Edmond de Rothschild, who made millions available for this purpose and established an organization to operate and administer the colonies. The difficulty encountered by practical Zionism in the slow progress of its colonization efforts gave rise to the intellectual re-assessment of Zionist aims by Ahad Ha'am in 1889, and a dramatic confrontation by Theodor Herzl in 1897. Together, these emphases ultimately converged to form the triad of the Zionist formula, practical, cultural and political.

Though recognizing the importance of the program in effect in his time, Ahad Ha'am demanded a spiritual awakening as a prerequisite. Without the latter, all effort was doomed to failure. He called upon the movement to concern itself with creed as well as deed, in the "preparation of the hearts" for the new cause.

In the meantime Zionist activity was sporadic—limited and frequently abortive—until Theodor Herzl and the eventful year of 1897, one of the most important dates in Jewish history. In 1894, Herzl, a brilliant Viennese journalist, while covering the dramatic Dreyfus trial in Paris, suddenly awoke to the hopeless and helpless position of the Jewish people. The victimized Dreyfus, in the role of scapegoat for the French military, epitomized the plight of his co-religionists. Out of soul-searching reflections there dawned upon Herzl the idea of a Jewish State as a haven of refuge and a pillar of strength, catapulting the Jews to the position of peer among the nations of the world. Toward this end, Herzl composed *The Jewish State* in 1896, and convened the first World Zionist Congress in Basle the following year. The manifesto, issued by the first international Jewish conclave, explicitly formulates the purpose of Zionism, henceforth indentified as the Basle Program: "Zionism seeks to secure for the Jewish people a publicly recognized, legally assured home in Palestine."[15]

Zionism now emerged as a world-wide organization seeking international recognition of its formal objectives. Herzl attracted Jewish dignitaries of Western Europe and set out on diplomatic missions to win over the heads of European governments, the Pope and the Sultan. His goal was a "charter" for Palestine. Seven anxious years of activity in the capitals of the world brought no immediate results so far as acquiring Palestine was concerned, but did focus the attention of government circles on the Zionist cause, and mobilized Jewish masses in service of the ideal. Herzl's diplomacy was pursued by his successors after his untimely death in 1904. These efforts finally culminated in the Balfour Declaration of 1917, issued by the British government, which was heralded as the first great victory for political Zionism.

The World Zionist Congress, assembled annually (and, after Herzl's death, biennially) became the platform on which Jews from all continents met, and from which the united articulate voice of Jewry spoke to the world. With the growth of the movement, a number of factions—or parties—were organized, unified in their loyalty to the Zionist ideal but differing in its interpretation. This diversification, crystallized throughout the decades, has been classified as follows:

(a) The Orthodox delegation led by Rabbi I. J. Reines (1839-1915) of Lithuania, formed the Mizrachi (abbreviation of the term for "spiritual center") party dedicated to the creation of a theocracy in Palestine constituting a religious Jewish community adhering to all the requirements of the traditional code of law—an ideal condition hitherto unattainable by a Jewish minority in a Gentile society.

(b) A liberal group headed by Leon Motzkin (1867-1933) designated itself as the "democratic faction". It was apprehensive of possible "clerical" domination and inclined toward an extensive cultural and social reconstruction. From this there later branched off the Socialist Zionist parties that played the decisive role in the rebuilding of Palestine, while others became identified as the General Zionists.[16]*

(c) After the First World War, the militant elements, regarding themselves as the true heirs to Herzl, became impatient with the slow progress of cautious diplomacy and the apparent watering down of Zionist aims. Under the banner of "Revisionism" they emerged as the vociferous champions of a Jewish State. The charismatic and controversial Vladimir Jabotinsky (d. 1940) was their dynamic leader. From their ranks came the extremist underground groups who undermined British rule in Palestine after World War II.

(d) The General Zionist, middle class elements uncommitted to any ism but dedicated to the general welfare of the people and the land of Israel—politically, philanthropically and economically—remained a loose federation of middle-of-the-roaders who represented the backbone of the Zionist movement and produced the recognized leaders. In

* See below.

America they have always been in the majority, and counted among them the outstanding personalities in the American Jewish community, such as Justice Brandeis.

III

While Herzlian Zionism was intensifying its diplomatic efforts, the "Second Wave of Immigration" to Palestine began in 1904. This brought the men who implemented the Zionist program and established the essential conditions for the birth of the State in 1948. From their ranks came the captains of the State, such as former Premier David Ben Gurion and the late president Yitzchak Ben Zvi. Moved by the positive factor in the vision of the Zionist ideal, and driven by the negative force of Russian pogroms of 1903-05, these men and women differed from the earlier pioneers of the 1880's by reason of their deeper social consciousness and realistic appraisal of conditions in Palestine. They came determined "to build and be rebuilt" after the fond hopes fed by the Russian revolution of 1905 had been dismally shattered. Upon arrival in Palestine they found that the earlier colonists, bereft of their initial idealism, and confronted by insurmountable difficulties, had compromised their Zionist principles by making expedient accommodations contrary to their avowed goals: the reliance on Arab labor and the philanthropy of Baron de Rothschild. The newcomers, *Chalutzim* (pioneers) as they were called, looked upon this as a parasitic existence, differing little from the old community in the "Holy Cities"—Jerusalem, Safed, Tiberias and Hebron—which subsisted upon collections by traditional agencies abroad. To the newcomers of the Second Immigration, Palestine was to be not only a change of venue but an opportunity for economic rehabilitation. A Jewish homeland, they insisted, could be built only by Jewish labor. Such ideas were not popular with the older settlers who considered menial work too degrading for respectable young men. The ensuing conflict became known as the struggle for "the conquest of labor".

The driving spirit of the age is reflected in the "Vitkin Manifesto", issued in 1906 by the Palestine teacher, Joseph Vitkin, as a call to Jewish youth in the diaspora to come to Palestine and pioneer its resettlement. Young people responded to the challenge and set out to create a new life in the old land. The document contains the basic motivation and fundamental principles of the faith and the mission of a new generation. It states that:

> The major causes of our blundering lie in our search for a short cut, our belief that the attainment of our goal is close at hand . . . and so we have turned with contempt from the harder road which is perhaps the surest, and in the end, the shortest. . . . Indeed, brothers, our strength is limited, though our purpose is high. For that very reason do not let us sit with our arms folded, if we still register the will to live. . . . We must work and struggle to redeem our land and fight with the courage of those for whom there is no possible retreat. . . . God forbid that we deceive ourselves, or the people whose cause we would champion, by describing the task as easy, the road as short. . . . Let us be fully aware that our ships are burned, that for us there is no other way in the whole world. . . . Know, brothers, your people is sick and unhappy. Accept from it no help, encouragement or reward. . . . Come rather to help and to awaken, and your greatest, your highest reward will be the realization of the vision itself. Hasten and come . . . for yet awhile longer, and we here . . . alone . . . shall perish.[17]

The right and duty of physical labor was supplemented by the imperative of self-defense. Plantations were usually guarded at night by hired Arabs, often in collusion with marauding bands. The new arrivals fought for and won the assignment to defend Jewish property by themselves. This, too, was a radical departure from the accepted patterns of behavior. The subjugated role of Jews in exile had prevented them from developing a tradition of self-defense when attacked by inciting mobs.

The friction between the settlers and the newcomers gradually led the *Chalutzim* to establish their own rural settlements, founded on principles conceived to uplift man and change society. The grim reality of the Palestine environment, combined with the social aspirations and idealistic yearnings of youthful enthusiasts, helped to evolve the idea of the collective upon which hundreds of Israel communities (*kibbutzim*) are still based. First of its kind, "mother of *kibbutzim*", was Degania, founded in 1909 on the eastern bank of the Jordan as it flows out of the Sea of Galilee.[18] The heart of the collective principle is voluntary economic communism for a select number of like-minded individuals who, joining together to reclaim the soil, share material goods, and form a harmonious relationship with each other. The unifying spirit is national redemption. A. D. Gordon, the intellectual leader of the movement, helped to formulate its methods and goals, embodied in his "religion of labor." It fostered an attitude of reverence for physical labor and communion with nature, in cognizance of the redeeming and spiritual powers of both. Meanwhile, the Zionist Congress had accepted the plan of Hermann Schapira, a German Jewish professor of mathematics, for a Jewish National Fund to purchase land in Palestine as the perpetual property of the Jewish people, leased to individual settlers who would be committed to work on the land without resorting to hired labor. Such a policy of national ownership was consonant, in part, with the collectivist aim of eliminating private property. Thus the seeds were planted for a Jewish homeland, in fulfillment of a vision aiming to solve the problems of the individual and the nation by a reconstructed society, free from the evils which attended European capitalism. The *kibbutz* setting was to answer not only national needs and resolve social problems, but also provide for personal fulfillment. The return to nature would have a beneficent effect upon the individual personality, restoring blessings long denied to urban Jewry. There was much of New England Transcendentalism, romantic nationalism, European Marxism and Rousseau's naturalism in this brand of Zionism, destined to pave the road to Jewish statehood, despite its starry-eyed utopianism.[19]

Simultaneous with diplomatic ventures in the evasive capitals of Europe, and physical and social pioneering in the inhospitable environment of Palestine, a cultural breakthrough of unparalleled dimensions was being achieved. Eliezer Ben Yehuda, by personal example and zealous dedication, engineered the resurrection of the Hebrew language after it had been consigned, for two millenia, to literary and religious usage alone. Ben Yehuda spelled out Zionism as a return to the language of the Hebrews as well as to their land.

IV

The outbreak of the World War in 1914 put a halt to further colonization and immigration. Non-Turkish citizens had to leave the country. Aaron Aaronson, brilliant young agronomist, descendent of early colonists, organized the secret spy ring *Nili* which provided valuable service to the British forces under General Allenby in the conquest of Palestine. Aaronson disappeared in 1919 under suspicious circumstances, while in flight from London to Paris on a British official plane.

Joseph Trumpeldor, veteran of the Russo-Japanese War, and later hero of self-defense in Palestine, together with Vladimir Jabotinsky, militant Zionist leader, organized Jewish units with recruits from all over the world including America. The Jewish Legion served with distinction, joining the Allies in the battle against the Turks. To assure full Jewish support for the cause of the Allies, the British government issued the Balfour Declaration in 1917, providing official endorsement of Zionist goals by a leading world power—the long sought aim of Herzlian Zionism. The Declaration reads:

> His Majesty's Government view with favour the establishment in Palestine of a national home for the Jewish people, and will use their best endeavours to facilitate the achievement of this object, it being clearly understood that nothing shall be done which may prejudice the civil and religious rights of existing non-Jewish communities in Palestine, or the rights and political status enjoyed by Jews in any other country.[20]

With the war over, there was considerable rehabilitation to be undertaken in Palestine. American Jewish agencies rushed to the aid of the decimated and impoverished community in Palestine, and along with European Jewish spokesmen, participated in the Versailles Peace Conference discussions on Jewish demands. In the final awarding of the Mandate to Britain, the Balfour Declaration was incorporated along with unequivocal stipulations on the task of Britain in Palestine. In addition to the text of the Balfour Declaration, the chief provisions include:

> Art. II—The Mandatory shall be responsible for the placing of the country under such political, administrative and economic conditions as will secure the establishment of the Jewish national home . . . and the development of self-

governing institutions, and also for safeguarding the civil and religious rights of all the inhabitants of Palestine, irrespective of race and religion.

Art. IV—An appropriate Jewish agency shall be recognized as a public body for the purpose of advising and cooperating with the Administration of Palestine. . . . The Zionist Organization, so long as its organization and constitutions are in the opinion of the Mandatory appropriate, shall be recognized as such agency. It shall take steps to secure the cooperation of all Jews who are willing to assist in the establishment of a Jewish national home.

Art. VI—The Administration of Palestine . . . shall facilitate Jewish immigration under suitable conditions and shall encourage in cooperation with the Jewish Agency . . . close settlement by Jews on the land. . . .[20]

As stated, the Zionist Organization received semi-governmental status to assist the Mandatory. An agreement had been publicly reached between Emir Feisel, leader of the Arabs, and Weizmann, on the mutual recognition of Jewish and Arab claims in the Near East with Palestine designated as the Jewish territory. The appointment by Britain of a Jew as High Commissioner in the person of Herbert Samuel turned out to be a curse in disguise, for in his desire to win over the Arabs, Samuel unwittingly harmed the Jewish cause. The Arabs were incited to mob violence in 1920, 1921 and again in 1929, with the hand of British authorities behind the incidents. Curtailment of Jewish immigration and colonization followed each outbreak. The twenty-eight years of British stewardship were studded with repeated British attempts to obstruct and liquidate the Mandate in official White Papers and in behind-the-scene machinations.

The upbuilding of the homeland continued in spite of all setbacks. Economic discrimination and political and religious oppression in Europe on the one hand and the Zionist ideal on the other brought hundreds of thousands—many of them through illegal channels—to the shores of the Holy Land. The Polish emigration of the twenties was followed by the influx of German Jews in the thirties. The Hebrew University on Mount Scopus in Jerusalem was founded in 1925 in an impressive ceremony that reverberated throughout the Jewish world. Previously, an issue of policy between rapid, massive resettlement advocated by the American Zionist leader and later Supreme Court Justice Brandeis, as against gradual colonization urged by Weizmann, was decided in favor of the latter at a stormy American Zionist convention in Cleveland in 1920. This led to modest but uninterrupted efforts at planned settlement with emphasis on young idealists from abroad drawn by choice rather than necessity. A "Labor Battalion" of itinerant volunteers undertook essential construction—particularly road-building—throughout the land. Pioneers struggled feverishly against malaria in the swamps of the Valley of Jezreel, succeeding valiantly in reclaiming the land from centuries of neglect. On the northern border, the previously mentioned Trumpeldor took up a last stand against Arab terrorists and, with his comrades, died in defense of Jewish soil, converting a remote outpost into a national symbol with himself as the revered hero, an inspiration to tens of thousands. After the government disbanded the Jewish battalions that helped to conquer Palestine, an underground defense army, *Hagana,* was formed. It trained the type of farmer-soldier upon whom the security of the Jewish population depended. In the thirties and especially during World War II, untold numbers were saved by the forces of the underground which outwitted the British blockade of Palestine shores. During the war the Zionist movement found itself in the paradoxical position of cooperating with Britain in the war against

Germany, and fighting British policy in Palestine. The Palestine Jewish community contributed significantly to the war effort in material and men. A Jewish Brigade once again distinguished itself in Europe. The men of the underground who had received their training and experience in the British Army, waited with exceptional patience while the civil population reacted with passive resistance to the repressive measures and the imprisonment of their leaders. Dissident elements, the *Irgun* and the Stern group, met violence with violence, making continued British rule untenable to masters and subjects alike, thereby catapulting the Palestine issue into a position of prominence in world public opinion and finally compelling the British government to place the matter before the United Nations.[21]

The 650,000 Jews of Palestine in 1948 were quite prepared for independence. They had a chain of semi-fortified colonies distributed throughout the country, an underground army, an officialdom of varied experience in public service, an organized labor movement, a modern economy and an established educational system. There was a tradition of heroic self-defense, astute diplomatic activity, sacrificial conquest of swamp and desert. There were the indigenous values of love of labor, social cooperation, solidarity with Jews abroad and last—but not least—a powerful religious motivation. They were fighting for freedom and survival and knew that world Jewry was behind them. By 1948, Palestine was no longer a controversial issue in Jewish life. With the exception of a fringe of upper class but insecure, peripheral Jews grouped into the American Council for Judaism, Zionists and non-Zionists shared responsibility through the Jewish Agency for Palestine, (organized in 1929), thereby creating a united front of worldwide Jewish support for Israel reborn.

The United Nations had voted the partition of Palestine into Jewish and Arab states in November, 1947. The independence of Israel was proclaimed on May 15, 1948. The armies of six Arab states—Egypt, Jordan, Saudi Arabia, Iraq, Syria, Lebanon—converged to destroy the infant State and crush the tiny community which they outnumbered in population one hundred to one.

Unaided by Western powers, which immediately announced an arms embargo, the Jews of Israel were assisted only by volunteers from abroad and their own "secret weapon"—the "no alternative" realization, the last hope for the survivors of the Nazi Holocaust. The hordes of invaders were defeated in the War of Liberation which took a costly toll in human life. The result of the War was a more geographically viable State as compared to the restrictive borders established by the United Nations. In 1956, and again in 1967, Arab terror and aggression were victoriously warded off. The Zionist dream of Israel united and Jerusalem restored, born with the destruction of the Second Commonwealth in 70 C. E., became a reality for two and a half million Jews living in Israel after the Six Day War of 1967.

With the establishment of the State, the political goal of the Zionist movement proclaimed in the Basle program of 1897 was fulfilled. Its continued function was dedicated to the preservation and re-inforcement of what had been achieved in Israel and to the unification of far-flung Jewry into a spiritual bond that would manifest solidarity with Zion rebuilt. An American Zionist leader has expressed the changed orientation of Zionism in these words:

> . . . We return to the first principle of Zionism. It is a principle which must be enunciated with greater emphasis than ever, now that the State of Israel has by its existence opened

> the way to implement it with full effect: the principle, namely, of the indivisible unity of our People; the identification therewith of Israel and World Jewry, the participation of Jews everywhere in the supreme experience of creating that ideal State which Herzl and his compeers foresaw from afar. . . . The establishment of Israel has not altered the spiritual objectives of Zionism, but in the nature of things it has created a shift in the scope and direction of our operations.[22]

The following chapters will trace the nature, origin and impact of these spiritual objectives in their initial formulation and subsequent crystallization in Israel society and education.

AN INSPIRED VISION

Moses Hess

I

IN THE SAME YEAR that an American president named Abraham issued a preliminary proclamation promising the emancipation of slaves in the coming year, a European Jewish intellectual named Moses published a book which planted the seeds for the national emancipation of the Jewish people in the promised land. *Rome and Jerusalem,* a book written in German by Moses Hess, appeared in 1862 and made its author the literary forerunner of the Jewish national ideal among occidental Jews. On the centenary of this first Zionist classic, the Government of Israel arranged for the reinterment of the author on the shores of the Sea of Galilee. This marked not only a tribute to a founding father of Zionism, but a testimony to the lasting influence of his book.

Hess's book was the first ambitious undertaking aimed at establishing the Jewish national movement upon sound philosophical foundations, with a practical program for their implementation. Simultaneous with expressed Zionist longings by scholarly rabbis and romantic speculations by Hebrew writers in Eastern Europe, Hess appeared as the apostle of the new Jewish nationalism among emancipated Jewry of Western Europe. The fact that a prominent spokesman of European socialism and the author of treatises in philosophy expounded Jewish nationalism marked a turning point in the nineteenth-century climate of opinion among Jews.

According to Hess's testimony, it was late in his life when he awoke to the needs of his people:

> After an estrangement of twenty years I am back with my people. I have come to be one of them again. . . .[23]

He was one of the first of the lost sheep to find his way home again after meandering about in distant pastures. The estrangement from Judaism was many years longer than indicated in the above-quoted confession. At the age of fifty, when he created the work which earned him a place in the hall of fame of Jewish notables, he already had behind him a long and illustrious career in revolutionary circles. His alienation from Jewish life reached back to his early manhood.

Born in Germany in 1812 to a pious and wealthy family, Hess was raised in a religious atmosphere. During his short stay at the Bonn University he became imbued with radical ideology, and he dedicated himself to its propagation. Breaking with his parents because of his revolutionary activities, he traveled aimlessly through England, France and Germany. A temporary reconciliation with his father improved his financial situation, but a permanent severance was soon brought about by his marriage to a gentile girl of ill repute.

Pursuing his socialistic and intellectual ventures, he wrote a number of philosophic books and treatises on economic-political and historical themes, and contributed extensively to radical publications. His independent thinking brought him into disfavor with Marx and Engels, as revealed in Marx's criticism leveled at him,[24] a fact which indicates the importance of Hess in radical quarters. This is further demonstrated by references to the ideas of Hess in one of Marx's early works.[25]

In 1848 Hess returned to Germany to take an active part in the revolution which subsequently failed. Condemned to death, he fled and finally found refuge in Paris where he continued to remain productive as a philosophical writer, an ardent socialist activist and, after the reawakening of his Jewish conscience, a champion of the national revival of his people. He died in 1875 at the age of 63.

II

In *Rome and Jerusalem* Hess contends that the spark of Jewish consciousness had been smouldering in his heart for twenty years, ever since the tragically notorious Damascus Affair of 1840 (based on a blood libel against Jews) attracted international attention and brought about the rude awakening of many assimilated Jews throughout the world. Hess comments on this in the Fifth Letter of his *magnum opus*:

> Twenty years ago, when an absurd and false accusation against the Jews was imported into Europe from Damascus, it evoked in the hearts of the Jews a bitter feeling of agony. Then it dawned upon me for the first time, in the midst of my socialistic activities, that I belong to my unfortunate, slandered, despised and dispersed people. And already, then,

> though I was greatly estranged from Judaism, I wanted to express my Jewish patriotic sentiment in a cry of anguish, but it was, unfortunately, immediately stifled in my heart by a greater pain which the suffering of the European Proletariat evoked in me.[26]

The record of the Hess conversion is not unique. The annals of Zionist history are studded with tales of repentant renegades, the zealous devotees of any number of current foreign fads, who suddenly were shocked into an awareness of their responsibilities to their own people. Their number included dignitaries who later graced international Zionist platforms, as well as many in the ranks of the movement who became the pioneers of the new Palestine. Hess is chronologically the first of this category in the Zionist "Who's Who".

It took an unusually long time for his initial reactions to crystallize into lasting and powerful sentiments. In addition to the Damascus Affair, there were two other factors to which the conversion of Hess is to be attributed. One was the struggle for "Free Italy" which led to the unification and liberation of most of the Italian peninsula by 1861. How much impact this had on Hess is evidenced by his insertion of the name *Rome* in the very title of his book, an obvious reference to the pending restoration of Italy's capital.

The next influence was the upsurge of nationalism throughout the subjected territories of Southern and Eastern Europe which planted the seed of Jewish national revival in many a sensitive Jewish soul.

Hess also asserted that his own intellectual maturation was responsible for his emerging Jewish convictions:

> . . . I discovered a real and strong relationship between my ethnological studies and the modern national movement.

> . . . These studies convinced me of the inevitable ultimate disappearance of any particular race dominance and the necessary regeneration of all oppressed peoples.[27]

Two elements in his mental development pointed in the same direction. As a socialist struggling against tyranny in any form, he demanded the liberation of oppressed classes and peoples, Israel not excepted. This was fortified by academic investigation into cultural and national characteristics and differences, suggesting an opportunity for the Jewish people to mold its own corporate *gestalt* and fulfill its destiny without interference. Cosmopolitanism, preaching fusion of nations into one undifferentiated humanity, he discovered to be totally unscientific. The new insight "became a dominating trait of my character and a lasting mood of my soul. No more did I seek to suppress the voice of my Jewish consciousness."[27]

III

What were the essentials of his philosophy of Jewish nationalism? A succinct statement of his views is condensed into one paragraph at the beginning of his *Rome and Jerusalem*.

> A thought which I believed to be forever buried in my heart has been revived in me anew. It is the thought of my nationality which is inseparably connected with the ancestral heritage and the memories of the Holy Land, the Eternal City, the birthplace of the belief in the divine unity of life, as well as the hope in the future brotherhood of men.[28]

Here is the forthright self-revelation of an emerging Zionist consciousness pervading an all-embracing philosophy of religion, history and culture. The nationalistic sentiments gripping him late in life were not isolated but were interwoven with a total *Weltanschauung* of cosmic, theological, historical and humanitarian ramifications. They were an inseparable aspect of his world view, fraught with universal significance beyond parochial interest.

Hess postulated a divine cosmic plan unfolding in time. The world is a unity; the same principles apply to nature and to society, joined by the unifying force of God.

The cosmic, organic and social are all subject to the genetic laws of progress operating consecutively in each of the three realms. The cosmic development, as recorded in the Bible, was followed upon its completion by organic evolution adequately traced in scientific investigations. Man's history, being comparatively recent, is destined to take the same course, ultimately leading to the full realization of the potentialities of harmony and fruition in social and spiritual achievement. The nineteenth century, marking the broadening of man's intellectual horizon and the liberation and regeneration of suppressed peoples, is the "springtime" of human history, ushering in a new age. Just as Palestine supplied a faith for mankind in the era of transition between antiquity and medieval times, similarly, in the present twilight before a new dawn, Israel—restored to its homeland—shall contribute to the regenerated spirit of man in the new era. At first, though hesitating to state explicitly this potential service to mankind (reserving the major liberating role to France as the "second homeland for all oppressed peoples"), Hess ultimately developed the argument to its logical conclusion:

> It is through Judaism that the history of humanity becomes a sacred history. I mean by that, that process of unified organic development which has its origin in the love of the

family, the members of which will be united by the holy spirit, the creative genius of history, as strongly as the organs of the body are united by the creative natural forces.[29]

The Jewish people . . . is still today, that organ of humanity which expresses the living creative force in universal history, mainly the organ of unifying and sanctifying love.[30]

The unique function of the Jewish people is to bring humanity toward a synthesis of materialistic and spiritual aims, destined to better the lot of mankind. This will be accomplished by translating the moral teachings of religion into the realities of daily living. Only then will the Jews fulfill their mission to society.

Israel can perform this service to mankind by setting an example on its own soil. From there, implementation of prophetic social justice will inspire emulation elsewhere:

Providence would not have prolonged your existence until today, had it not reserved for you the holiest of all missions. The hour has struck for the resettlement on the banks of the Jordan. The historical books of the royal prophets can, perhaps, be written again only by you.[31]

The rebirth of Israel is inevitable to anyone who understands the signs of the times.

The old frame-work of European society, battered so often by the storms of revolution, is cracking and groaning on all sides. It can no longer stand the storm.

Just as after the last catastrophe of organic life, when the historical races came into the world's arena, there came their division into tribes, and the position and the role of the latter was determined, so after the last catastrophe in social life, when the spirit of humanity shall have reached

> its maturity, will our people, with the other historical peoples, find its legitimate place in universal history.[32]

Return to Palestine, therefore, will come not only as a result of the dialectical processes of history; it will come because it is a spiritual necessity in order that the Jews may assume the role which is their destiny in civilization. In its dispersion, the Jewish people is unable to carry out this mission because of abnormal economic conditions, a deteriorated Jewish cultural situation, and the inhibiting social status. National independence in Palestine will deliver them from plight and release the powers of rejuvenation, enabling them to discharge their assumed obligation to the peoples of the world. In its renewed exalted capacity the Jewish people, restored to its homeland, appears as "the triumphal arch of the future historical epoch, under which the great covenant of humanity will be written and sealed. . . ."[33] Hess therefore adopted the mission concept fundamental to Reform Judaism, but reinterpreted it to apply to a reconstituted Jewish nation in the Land of Israel. A few years after the appearance of his major work, he returned to the theme in his "Letters on the Mission of Israel in the History of Mankind."[34]

> . . . for our people is destined to fulfill a role in history other than the one dreamt of for fifty years, by those who are preoccupied with reforming our religion.

This will be made possible with the revival of the Jewish people as a nation planted on its own soil.

The call of the hour, in preparing for the rebirth of the Jewish nation, is to keep alive this hope and reawaken it where it slumbers. What is required is constant vigilance and readiness to take advantage of an international situation conducive to the restoration of a Jewish State. Political alertness, however, is inadequate unless it is "preceded by colonizing ventures,"[35] a formula anticipatory of the Zionist program of later decades.

Hess envisioned the spiritual revival of Judaism following on the heels of a reconstituted, numerically significant community in the Land of Israel. He endorsed the colonization plan advocated by the contemporary Rabbi Kalisher, urging solicitation of leading Jewish financiers for this project, and pointed to existing conditions favorable to the recognition of Jewish aims. He believed that France's involvement in the building of the Suez Canal could sway her, if sufficient influence were brought to bear, toward sponsoring Jewish resettlement in Palestine under French protection. This idea of viewing the international political arena with an eye to gaining assistance from western powers later became a most important plank in the Zionism of Theodor Herzl, architect of the World Zionist Organization, and eventually culminated in the Balfour Declaration of the British Government during the First World War.

A word is in order concerning emancipation of Jews in Europe generally. Citizenship rights were first granted to Jews by the French Revolution in 1791. Though these rights were somewhat curtailed by Napoleon, his military conquests brought relief to Jews in other countries. Then, when the victors in the Napoleonic wars convened for the Congress of Vienna, in 1815, they deprived most Jews of their newly acquired status.

The upsurge of reaction led many to conversion in order to escape the fate of their fellow Jew. A more positive program, designed to refute the specious arguments against emancipation by modifying and modernizing Jewish religious thought and practice, was undertaken by the Reform movement in Germany. However, it was not satisfied with external reforms prompted by aesthetic considerations, as initially contemplated by its founders, but struck at the very heart of religion by eliminating the Hebrew language and all references to Zion found in the prayer book. Simultaneously, many intellectuals were becoming zealous devotees of the new nationalism of their respective countries. The nascent nationalism was comprehensive in scope and frequently demanded considerable retreat from religious convictions as proof of meriting equal rights. This was especially true in Germany. Responding to the challenge in an over-ardent fashion, many Jews were ready to make the necessary concessions. Actually, the weakening of Jewish bonds had little to do with the final emancipation of West European Jewry by a series of legislative enactments from 1830 to 1870, essentially motivated by political, economic and democratic considerations. In Eastern Europe equal rights were not granted until after the first World War.[36]

IV

Thus two roads led to Zion from two directions during the nineteenth century. One was positive, paved with the desire for unhampered religious and cultural expression which had been inhibited under the pressure of a dominating majority civilization. The other was negative, leading out of the need to flee the scourge of anti-Semitism. The trail-blazers of the Zionist ideal traversed either path. Though Hess reacted very strongly to anti-Semitism among his fellow socialists and to hostilities against Jews elsewhere, he was moved mainly by spiritual considerations as already indicated. The return to Palestine meant to him a challenge and an opportunity for the unfolding of the Jewish spirit. Anticipating much of the Zionist political platform that was subsequently more clearly enunciated by his successors, he represented the embryonic stage of a philosophy of spiritual rebirth evolved by Ahad Ha'am and others. In the messianic role he assigned to the resurrected Jewish nation, Hess reached to inspired ethereal heights beyond the grasp of many of his heirs—the theoreticians and architects of the national rebirth.

Hess perceived the profound truth that assimilation never mitigates the injuries of anti-Semitism, but frequently aggravates them from without and weakens the psychological immunity from within. The process of assimilation incurs a loss of respect on the part of the non-Jew and diminishes the emotional protectiveness of the Jew himself. He claimed that the bond of peoplehood does not interfere with loyalty to one's country. History contains many examples of how Jewish identification and patriotic allegiance to one's country have existed harmoniously and with mutual reinforcement.

> . . . it is possible to be a good, patriotic national Jew, in the full sense of the word, and at the same time participate in the cultural and political life of the land . . .[37]

Central in the critical perspective of Hess was the road of assimilation embarked upon by occidental Jewry. The merciless denunciation which he levelled at its philosophy of denial of the national historical elements in the Jewish religion, he also directed against the Reform movement itself. The religious reform sparked by the expressed desire to modernize the religious tradition, he regarded as a fiasco which emasculated the faith and transformed it into a sterile creed. He accused his emancipated co-religionists of apish behavior unbecoming to men of dignity. To reject trans-national identification with the Jewish people in favor of vague theological commitments was too great a price for men of honor to pay for civil rights. He dramatically cried out: "If it were true that Jewish emancipation in exile is incompatible with Jewish nationality, then it were the duty of the Jews to sacrifice the former for the sake of the latter."[38] The sacrifice of integrity and conviction, cowardly offered by many on the altars of emancipation, was the butt of attacks by Hess. He scornfully ignored and pitied those renegades who sought refuge in total conversion, noting that in the new racial anti-Semitism baptism made little difference.

Critical as Hess was of Reform, he could not at the same time fully agree with Orthodoxy. Its formalism and rigidity made it unpalatable, though he subjected it to a less severe judgment than he did Reform. The former lacked an articulate national consciousness, while the latter tried to suppress it. His reading of the newly-published Jewish history volumes of Graetz inspired him with an appreciation of the spiritual development of Judaism and love of his people. He could then say that,

> the main problem of the Jewish national movement is . . . how to awaken the patriotic sentiments in the hearts of our progressive Jews, and how to liberate the Jewish masses, by means of this patriotism, from a spirit of deadening formalism.[39]

He was not discouraged by apparent unconcern on the part of both camps. A tremendous struggle would have to be undertaken before admitting defeat in that "the Jewish heart is dead . . . no more capable of patriotic inspiration."[39] His was a fond hope for a third position on the religious front, removed from Reform negation, yet not too close to ossified Orthodoxy. This possibility materialized with the rise of Conservative Judaism, which occurred after his demise. Hess entertained such hope for

Palestine, where "there will rise in the Holy Land . . . universities conducted by able scholars whose spirit will . . . harmonize with the ancient Jewish national religion."[40]

Hess did not abandon socialism when he turned to Jewish nationalism. His entire messianic philosophy was predicated upon a new Jewish society established on the foundation of labor, setting the example for better relations between capital and labor. The materialism of Marx alienated him from the start, but idealistic socialism captured his imagination. It formed an integral part of the pattern of cosmic and social regeneration which he had outlined. The partnership of Socialism and science would eventually establish a better order. The Jewish people would certainly contribute in its own land to the "unity of different tendencies of social life into one center of activity."[41]

More than a quarter of a century after the death of Hess, pioneers streaming to the shores of Palestine raised aloft the banner he had earlier held, not always aware of Hess who had antedated them.

V

What effect did Hess's preaching have on his contemporaries? The response was mostly negative. Angered by his outspoken eloquence, "the assimilationist camp aims all its political arrows at the man who dared to negate the accepted catechism of assimilation."[42] In his own day Hess seems to have lost the battle in spite of his continued efforts in the same direction after the publication of his book. Over the years he was rediscovered as a prophet of the Jewish national renaissance, and *Rome and Jerusalem* became a source of inspiration to many. His other extensive political and historical writings, to which he had devoted the greater part of his life and talents, were relegated to oblivion.[43]

Nearly all the tenets of Zionism received their earliest formulation from Hess. He advocated political Zionism before Herzl, dreamed of spiritual and cultural resurgence before Ahad Ha'am, protected socio-economic reconstruction before Syrkin and Borochov, and hinted at religious rejuvenation before the advent of men of kindred spirit in America. All this was tinted with the messianic glow of universal relations and eternal values, elevating and charging the Jewish national revival to an exalted position of humanitarian and spiritual dimensions.

Hess's influence upon Israel society today was channeled through others. His ideas were rediscovered and developed by the Zionist men of thought and letters of a later generation, through whose medium they were absorbed in the institutions and values of the emerging society in Israel. Time has vindicated most of his conclusions, even though

> his book was forgotten . . . until the Zionist movement of Russia and Poland came and raised Hess and his book from the depths of oblivion and set him up among the prophets of Zionism and the founders of its teachings.[44]

As a primary source of inspiration Hess still points to: the bankruptcy of assimilation, the messianic aspects of Zionism, the social reconstructionist ideals of the Jewish national movement, the regenerative function of Jewish spiritual creativity, the true meaning of emancipation in terms of human dignity and national character, the possibility of a religious revival attuned to the modern scene and the fusion of universal socialism with national aspirations.

SPIRITUAL NATIONALISM

Peretz Smolenskin

I

THE LAST hundred and fifty years of Jewish life may be conveniently and equally divided into the age of Enlightenment and the age of National Revival. Though the Enlightenment, as an organized movement aiming to bring Western culture and modernization to Jewish life and thought, began with Moses Mendelssohn in Berlin by the middle of the eighteenth century, it didn't reach Russian Jewry, the largest Jewish community, until half a century later.

Designating the prevailing pattern up to the year 1800 as the "thesis," the men of *Haskala* (Enlightenment) propelled toward an "antithesis," while the generation of Revival reverted to a "synthesis." At first, the pendulum swung from religious particularism to opportunistic universalism, and from isolationist pedanticism to cultural assimilationism. Then nationalism linked the group-solidifying tendency of the old with the intellectualism of the new.

The man who himself passed through all these stages, contributing more than any other person to the rise of the philosophy of Jewish nationalism, was the Hebrew novelist, essayist and editor, Peretz Smolenskin. In performing this function, he is regarded in Hebrew letters as the father of the national ideal.

Smolenskin was born in 1840 into a poverty stricken household in White Russia. He had an unhappy youth. His family lived in constant fear of virulent anti-Semitism and had to flee for their lives. A young brother was kidnapped as a child—a victim of the prevailing system of recruiting Jewish boys for twenty-five years of army service. His father died, and at the age of eleven Peretz had already been sent away from home to study at a *yeshiva*. Expelled for reading banned books, (a category including everything which was not part of the curriculum) he sought refuge in the sectarian, pietistic environment of a Hassidic miracle-rabbi. He became a member of wandering cantorial choirs, an itinerant preacher, and a private Hebrew tutor, finally settling in Odessa at the age of twenty-two.

Free to indulge in "enlightenment" in a cosmopolitan modern city, Smolenskin began a career of creative writing in Hebrew. After moving to Vienna, beyond reach of the Russian censor, he issued the monthly *Hashahar* ("The Dawn"), which ushered in the dawn of a new era in Hebrew thought and literature. He published seven novels and a few books of essays, suffering constantly from economic hardship and poor health while enjoying unsurpassed popularity among the younger generation. He continued to engage in various polemics despite physical deterioration, and in 1885 he died of tuberculosis at the age of forty-five. His publication *Hashahar* ceased with its editor's demise, but the ideas it planted took root and blossomed.

II

The story of Smolenskin's intellectual growth is an integral part of the history of modern Jewish thought. At the beginning of Smolenskin's career as a writer, two ideologies were struggling for supremacy within the Jewish community. Orthodoxy was equating loyalty to Judaism with conventional standards of appearance and garb, the traditional curriculum and numerous folkways indigenous to the ghetto. Pitched against it was Europe-infatuated *Haskala*, offering—as a panacea for all ills affecting the Jew—secular studies, external modernization and modified cultural assimilation. The Russian movement, unlike its German antecedent, found itself paradoxically fostering a flourishing Hebrew literature while simultaneously advocating a program of cultural assimilation as a substitute for protective withdrawal and isolation. Actually, protagonists of *Haskala* were confusing modernization with cultural integration, failing to realize that identifying a secular Hebrew literature with the first was not necessarily the same as achieving the second. The novelist, Smolenskin—in contrast to the essayists of later years—originally followed the *Haskala* stereotype, distinguishing sharply between the "enlightened" hero and the Orthodox villain. After living in Vienna, he altered his perspective. There he was able to gain direct, uncolored impressions of "enlightened" Jews. What was acclaimed in the new form was as distasteful to him as that which he had condemned in the old.

If he started out by objecting to the religious superstition, social corruption and intellectual suppression of the old Synagogue, he now protested vehemently against the superficiality, materialism and ignorance of Judaism which were rampant in the salons of the moderns. He began to realize that the liberated Jew, taught to ascribe inferiority and anachronism to his own heritage, while attributing superiority and progress to the Christian culture, hardly proved the paragon of virtue and dignity he was intended to be.

Smolenskin now launched an offensive against the two opposing camps through the journal which he edited, proofread, half filled with his own articles and stories, printed, managed and distributed personally. He made it into a forceful medium for an awakened national consciousness.

The statement of policy which introduced the new publication is a bold proclamation of challenging ideas that later became the fighting program of the new era:

> We shall be as other nations in cherishing our tongue and our people's honor. We are not ashamed of our faith in the ultimate end of exile, when the day shall come and dominion shall return to the House of David. . . . We shall not blush as we hold on to the ancient tongue which accompanied us from nation to nation, and in which our poets and seers sang.[45]

Smolenskin developed his theory of Jewish survival in his book entitled *Am Olam* ("An Eternal People"). Therein he defined Jews as "a nation of the spirit," unencumbered by geographic, political and linguistic features required by other nations. He accepted in essence the basic premise of the assimilationist school which divorced Jewishness from its traditional attachment to land and language; but he rejected its conclusion that Judaism is a mere doctrinal bond among members of different nationalities sharing a common faith. On the contrary, he maintained, the national ties uniting dispersed Jewry are stronger than the political, geographic and linguistic denominators solidifying other peoples. Jews have outgrown these forms in their spiritual evolution. The common faith by itself is not an unchanging set of dogmas, but rather intellectual endeavor and the priority of the spiritual. The unity of Israel was preserved in exile long after expulsion from the homeland, a condition which deprived it of the usual characteristics of nationhood. Its destiny is to pursue its mission among the nations without losing its identity manifested in these higher traits of peoplehood.

Here again is a concept borrowed from the classical Jewish Reform philosophy of early nineteenth century Germany. Nevertheless, the common ground shared with the assimilationist point of view becomes the fertile soil for the sprouting of nationalism. The two negations of Reform Judaism regarding the hope of national redemption, and the primacy of Hebrew language, are paramount affirmations in Smolenskin's thought. They are indispensable in the preservation and reinforcement of the spiritual nation which must retain its unity and identity in order to serve a noble purpose. The nationalism of Jews, being different in kind from the nationalism of others, cannot, therefore, stand in the way of emancipation. The assumption that a nation will not grant equal rights to members of an alien minority insisting upon its own distinctiveness is not tenable. The modern age is bound to recognize it and accept not only the individual Jew but also the Jewish people for what it is. Due recognition of the uniqueness of Jewish peoplehood, combined with a constructive program for the revival of Hebrew culture, spiritual values and the messianic hope, will present an effective deterrent to the corroding effects of assimilation.

> For the children of Israel have existed longer than other people because they considered themselves a people of the

> spirit, and were so labelled by all their scholars, authors and seers. . . .
>
> Indeed we are a people, we are a people from ancient times to this day! We never ceased being a people when our kingdom was destroyed and we were exiled from our land. And nothing which will ever occur will prevent us from remaining a people. Of course, we differ from other nations, just as we differed from them when we dwelt in our land, in not being dependent upon state and country. For we were always a nation of the spirit whose Law preceded land and state.[46]

This national feeling should be cultivated by the modern Jew. The unity of the Jewish people throughout the world will be maintained

> by reviving the Hebrew tongue and placing it in the mouths of all Israelites desiring to remain Israelites; for besides being the binding cord for all of us, it is a monument to our ancestors of ancient days. . . . On it we place our hope for unity in the days to come when we shall have succeeded in building a home.[47]

Remaining true to the messianic faith of ages, Smolenskin is not prepared to abandon the hope for returning to the Land of Israel. As for the immediate future, Smolenskin suggests that the new Jew will be bilingual, adopting the language of his residence for his practical and secular activities and acquiring mastery of historical Hebrew for spiritual and intellectual purposes, a policy maintained officially in Jewish historical experience ever since the dispersion at the dawn of the Christian era. Hebrew, destined to serve in an exalted role, is not a revived vernacular but the heritage of great books and ideas of the past, and continued literary creativity in the present.

Smolenskin was among the first to recognize the real dangers of the Enlightenment movement in Germany and its successor in Eastern Europe. He was not opposed to religious change, as determined by the needs of the people. Nor was he critical of the aesthetic emphasis of Reform. But the emasculation of Jewish theology which eliminated the components of Hebrew language, messianic return to Zion and world Jewish unity, he diagnosed as false and dangerous, in violation of the fundamental spirit of Judaism and detrimental to its survival. It instilled a sense of inferiority without pointing the way to improvement on the road to self-acceptance. It weakened the bonds necessary to keep a landless people together.

At the same time Smolenskin observed that the promise of the Enlightenment for better relations with the non-Jew would prove a mirage. He appealed for abandoning "the ideals of *Haskala* and the folly of their acts . . . honor our people and the remnant of our refuge before it is too late."[48] He viewed the *Haskala* as a destructive force inimical to national interests. Instead of heeding the ancient prophetic call to foresake the ways of the surrounding nations, the leaders of the *Haskala* inverted the criticism to achieve the opposite. In the attack upon the Jewish reformation he may have been influenced by Hess, whose book, *Rome and Jerusalem,* preceded Smolenskin by nearly two decades. The initial motivation, however, was different: not the challenge of anti-Semitism as in Hess, but the threat of loss of the Jewish character and ultimate national disintegration. He was concerned with spiritual survival rather than physical preservation.

Smolenskin's very preoccupation with this issue was a pioneer venture. Prior to him, the question most frequently posed by those concerned with the Jewish problem was how to improve the physical lot of the Jews. Smolenskin introduced the issue of preserving Judaism, which entailed defining its nature and projecting a program for its reinforcement. He attempted to supply both. Analyzing Smolenskin's philosophy, a distinguished scholar of the twentieth century summarizes his initial doctrine as

> not one of redemption but of diaspora nationalism. Unlike Hess, he is not a "Zionist" . . . Only later does he become one of the founders of Zionism. . . . In his first period he was spiritual-disapora-centered. . . . Smolenskin created the concept of the spiritual nation.[49]

III

When crisis confronted Russian Jewry in the early eighties, shattering the hopes of Enlightenment in the sweeping wave of anti-Jewish terror, Smolenskin felt that he had sufficiently prepared his public for the necessary reorientation. Unlike other intellectuals whose philosophy crumbled in the ruins of Jewish communities, he did not have to seek a new ideology. As an advocate of diaspora nationalism he was ready for the next step, the second stage of his productive deliberations—the ideal of Zionism. Though hesitant at first, when in 1878 his own monthly printed a proposal by Eliezer ben Yehuda for a return to Palestine, he now openly preached the Zionist message. He levelled severe criticism at the French Jewish agency, Alliance Israélite Universelle, for failing to divert its public funds to the support of immigration to Palestine. He vehemently opposed allocating the charity funds for financing immigration to America:

> Needless to prove that it would be in the best interest of the refugees coming from one land, to reconvene as a group in another. . . . There is no better place for them to turn to than the land of Israel.[50]

He vigorously campaigned toward this end, but with no success. The leaders of French Jewry were deaf to the rising voice of national sentiment for the ancient homeland.

The call for expediting a mass return to the Holy Land was not motivated by practical considerations alone. Smolenskin became an enthusiastic protagonist of the idea of national redemption attended by spiritual revival. In consonance with his previous emphasis upon the spiritual characteristic of Jewish nationhood, he envisioned its reinforcement by the emergence of a national center:

> Our unity and existence are dependent upon the ideal of the Land of Israel. If a number of families will gather in one location, that location will become the center for the Law of the nation, and from thence shall come forth the Law for all the lands.[51]

Thus the originator of an advanced extra-territorial nationalism, unattached to conventional attributes, is compelled by the pressure of events to retreat to the firm ground of an independent territory. It seems that even a *spiritual* nation should have a *physical* home. Smolenskin had embarked upon a new path, opening up wide vistas on the road to Zion.

Hence, the most popular novelist of the *Haskala* generation became the publicist who championed a resurgent nationalism, leading to Zionism. The prolific author of fiction,[52] exposing the humiliation and deterioration of ghetto life, became the essayist who mercilessly revealed the bankruptcy of modernism and emancipation, finally emerging as the protagonist of the new nationalism.

There were others before him who had called for a return to Palestine. These offered reinterpretations of the Orthodox position within the traditional camp. Some represented the mystic, poetic yearnings of neophytes like Hess.

Neither type exerted much influence upon an awakened generation of young people captivated by the glitter and glamour of European civilization. It was Smolenskin, in his spirited and multifarious writings, who stimulated the minds and animated the spirit, paving the way for Zionist societies in the years following the pogroms of 1881. He himself was active organizationally in Vienna, where he founded the first student Zionist group, *Kadima,* which fifteen years later was so receptive to Herzl's Zionist program. He also played an active role in similar ventures as a nascent Zionist movement gained momentum.

Smolenskin's secular nationalism, devoid of theological trappings but founded on spiritual values, became a dynamic, inspirational message, developed and defined in succeeding decades of Zionist debate. It contained an interpretation of history, a critical appraisal of the combatant forces of his day and an articulate program of cultural reconstruction. No preceding or contemporary Jewish writer of the nineteenth century reached such a large number and enjoyed such a loyal following. The pathos and vigor of his style, the power of his expression, the originality and integrity of his reflection, all served to make him a commanding figure on the literary scene. An outstanding historian in Israel regards Smolenskin as

> the greatest author-warrior of modern Hebrew literature. . . . More than a writer, he was the standard-bearer of a new ideal. If we assume that literary creations can plant and nourish national and social forces originally brought into being by vital historic causes . . . and accepted by virtue of their taking on form and content in great literary works—then we have the right to consider the new national ideal of Israel and the Zionist ideal based on it, as well as its product, the State of Israel, to a large measure the product of Peretz Smolenskin.[53]

At least two leading figures in modern Jewish thought borrowed heavily from Smolenskin. The theory of "diaspora nationalism," expounded by the Jewish historian Simon Dubnow, which became the political platform of an organized sector in the East European Jewish community, appears to have much in common with Smolenskin's pre-Zionist ideas. Smolenskin's concept of a world Jewish people, united by a spiritual bond without a geographic center, received practical application in Dubnow's plan of autonomous communities. It was Smolenskin who first presented Dubnow's case for the "advanced" nationalism of the Jewish people which, unlike the nationalism of others, requires no single territorial base.

Ahad Ha'am's penetrating analysis of the spiritual plight of occidental Jewry was aided considerably by Smolenskin's critique of the German *Haskala* and Reform ideology. Hebrew culture, as the chief instrumentality in the Jewish "spiritual revival" throughout the world, is a concept originally promulgated by Smolenskin and later developed by Ahad Ha'am.

On the American Jewish scene, Mordecai Kaplan, founder of the Reconstructionist movement, in his emphasis upon living in two cultures—the American and the Jewish—also draws on Smolenskin's initial advocacy of bilingualism in Jewish life.

In the final appraisal, Smolenskin stands for concepts that have not lost their meaningfulness in present day Israel. Significant are the ideas of (a) a secular nationalism linked to spiritual values, charging it with ethical and intellectual implications; (b) a flourishing Hebrew culture, unifying and elevating the scattered tribes of Jewry; (c) a healthy appreciation of the Jewish heritage with little sympathy for unchecked infiltration of alien standards and institutions, though with ample recognition of positive contributions by others; (d) an affirmation of the existence of a Jewish people beyond the borders of Israel, joined together in a spiritual bond.

Mention has already been made of the fact that Moses Hess, writing in German, antedated Peretz Smolenskin's Hebrew messages. But Hess was a voice lost in the din of rushing events. Smolenskin's call reached a public which continued to be influenced by him long after his earthly departure. Then came Ahad Ha'am who accepted the basic concepts of Smolenskin, erecting upon them the elaborate structure of Cultural Zionism.

The late Professor Klausner of the Hebrew University may have been correct in nominating Smolenskin as the father of the national ideal, and the first among the builders who laid the foundation for the State of Israel.[53]

AUTO-EMANCIPATION

Leon Pinsker

I

In 1882, a thirty-page pamphlet, written in German, aroused Jewish public opinion to an unprecedented degree, and established its author among the most important of the founding fathers of Zionism. The essay was called *Auto-Emancipation,* written by a sixty-one-year-old Russian Jewish doctor named Leon Pinsker. Though locally prominent in Odessa as a benevolent and highly qualified physician, Pinsker hitherto had kept himself remote from Jewish nationalistic circles. For a number of years he had been actively identified with an organization that promoted Russian culture among Jews. It was only during his sunset years that he turned away from his trodden path to pave a new road to Zion. This conversion from assimilationist to nationalist convictions is integrally related to nineteenth century events in the epic story of Zionism.

"Enlightenment" came late to the compact Jewish masses of the Russian empire. It drew its nourishment from three sources, two authentic and one spurious, and in less than a century it ran its course from inception to recession. A sincere thirst for knowledge impelled certain adventuresome spirits to drink deeply from the fountains of European learning and Biblical scholarship (the latter, strangely enough, having been excluded from required orthodox studies.) This avid pursuit was made doubly alluring by the mirage of civil rights that offered a future reward to a deserving "enlightened" community. The naive faith in an illusory panacea for all socio-economic ills was encouraged by a government which secretly hoped that Enlightenment would eventually lead in the direction of assimilation and conversion to Christianity.

Pinsker had the good fortune to be raised in a home environment which combined European culture with Jewish tradition. Unlike many of his contemporaries, he was therefore spared the emotional strain of breaking away from the old world. His father was a prominent intellectual who made significant contributions to Jewish scholarship. Young Pinsker's early education included Jewish and secular studies, followed by medical school. He became a popular doctor, known for his generosity to the poor without concern for monetary compensation. While pursuing advanced studies in German and Austrian universities, he became acquainted with the chief exponents of religious reform and cultural assimilation, and was duly influenced by them. After returning home, he easily drifted toward those peripheral circles of the Jewish community who desired to improve the lot of their co-religionists by a process of Russification. In Odessa, the most modern city of the Czar's empire, this experiment took on a more extreme form when the "Organization for Enlightenment" advocated substituting Russian for Hebrew in worship, following in the footsteps of German Reform.

Toward this end they issued a journal and planned to organize elementary schools. Pinsker was actively espousing the publicly announced program of

> total assimilation with the ruling community—the Messiah which our enlightened and better public awaits. . . . Thus there is no need for separate community agencies nor special schools with their own curriculum, and certainly there is no need for a different language.[54]

In later years he referred to this former mood as one characterising

> . . . those misty-eyed idealists belonging to that church which placed freedom, equality and fraternity as the supreme dogma. I also believed in the victory of progress of eighteenth century humanism. I was confident of its triumph and that Europe would fully consent to grant us equal rights.[55]

II

Then the crisis came, and the Jewish intelligentsia lost its bearings until its course was rechartered in another direction. An ominous prelude to the storm that swooped down a decade later was staged in 1871 when the first Russian pogrom of the century broke out in Odessa. It came as a surprise, temporarily interfering with the mood of increasing confidence in the efficacy of Enlightenment. One spokesman for the assimilationist camp confessed that "the leaders of the Odessa chapter have been forcibly convinced that all efforts at joining with the Russian residents are to no avail."[56]

Pinsker, too, was taken aback. The very foundation of assimilation—that it makes for greater acceptance by gentiles—was shaken. The "Organization for Enlightenment" was disbanded, but after a few years it was reconvened and began functioning anew. The assumption was that local atrocities represented isolated incidents.

Then, for all practical purposes, the Odessa episode became national policy. On the heels of the assassination of Alexander II in 1881, a wave of mob violence against Jews swept through Russia, with the passive or even active complicity of all strata of society. The death knell for assimilationist philosophy was sounded when a bewildered Jewish intelligentsia suddenly found itself, as the emperor in the fairy tale, without any clothes. Homeless throngs streamed across the borders on the way to America. Some turned their eyes toward Palestine. On the ruins of a discredited ideology, the Zionist banner was quickly and independently hoisted in many places. Pinsker himself recognized how helpless Jews were in their current state, and how hopeless were the chances for improving their doleful lot within the existing framework. He was convinced of the unquestionable need for a change of location as a basis for better conditions. His analysis of the Jewish problem, in light of the new emergency, and the recommended solution, were presented in the aforementioned pamphlet published in 1882. It was written in German as an epistle to the more influential and affluent Jews of Western Europe in order to convince them of the fallacies of the emancipation theory and induce them to cooperate with his constructive substitute program.

The reaction abroad to Pinsker's manifesto was mostly negative. At home, however, where it was immediately translated into Hebrew, Russian and Yiddish, the effect was overwhelming. The newly organized *Hovevei Zion* ("Lovers of Zion") groups, formed for the purpose of Jewish colonization activity in Palestine, looked up to him as their new leader. Their first national conference, convening in the Silesian town of Katowitz (since political gatherings were illegal in Russia), established its national organization in 1884 with Pinsker as its head. He served in that capacity until his death in 1891 at the age of seventy, faithfully devoting himself to fund-raising projects in support of the Palestine colonists, and the slow and tedious tasks of propagating the Zionist ideal. Up to the time of his death he upheld the morale and preserved the unity of the scattered Zionist societies in Russia which operated in secret until legalized in 1890.

III

> It was not because Pinsker became the leader of *Hibat Zion* that he holds his place in our story. . . . He was a man of stainless character, lofty idealism, and deep convictions, but he was unable to cope with the external forces that impeded the movement, nor with the internal conflicts that bedeviled it. Pinsker was not a great leader but a great apostle, and he owes his place in the story of Zionism to his *Auto-Emancipation*. . . .[57]

Pinsker's only published work, *Auto-Emancipation,* is a Russian Jew's appeal to his own people. The name is significant. Emancipation, as the treasured acquisition of occidental Jewry, represented not only equality before the law, with the ensuing social privileges, but also human dignity of immeasurable psychological import. Pinsker claimed, however, that it was an inadequate surrogate both for the westerners who had achieved it and the easterners aspiring toward it. It solved the Jewish problem theoretically and superficially instead of realistically and adequately. The ills of anti-Semitism, infecting European society throughout, remained unabated by the medicinal powers of Enlightenment. Only self-emancipation, in terms other than hitherto subscribed to, offered a solution.

The author perceived that nations, without exception, do not regard Jews as they do other minorities. Aliens enjoy a status based upon the existence of a fatherland elsewhere, capable of reciprocating in sundry ways the treatment meted out to its sons on foreign soil. Jews who lack normal characteristics of nationhood, are not extended similar consideration.

> The Jewish people has no fatherland of its own, though many motherlands; no center of focus or gravity, no government of its own, no official representation. They home everywhere but are nowhere at home. The nations have never to deal with a Jewish nation, but always with mere Jews.[58]

The peculiar circumstances of the Jewish people elicit fear and suspicion in the hearts of gentiles who behold "the ghostlike apparition of a living corpse of a people no longer alive . . . walking among the living without precedence in history."[59] The fears and prejudices culminate in the socially hereditary disease of "Judeophobia." It is, therefore, futile to contend against these hostile tendencies, since prejudice as an emotional reaction cannot be erased by the rational process of logical argumentation. Other factors, such as economic competition, aggravate the situation, for no one in his own home welcomes competition by a stranger. Different classes ascribe to the Jew characteristics most unsavory from their own point of view, with the result that Jews supposedy assume mutually contradictory roles, all of them odious:

> . . . to the living the Jew is a corpse, to the native a foreigner, to the homesteader a vagrant, to the proprietary a beggar, to the poor an exploiter and a millionaire, to the patriot a man without a country, for all a hated rival.[60]

Emancipation merely scratches the surface, failing to cope with the pathological and economic aspects of the problem. As a legal concession, it offers a palliative but never a remedy, for it cannot remove the stigma of homelessness from the Jew to exonerate and rehabilitate him in the sight of mankind.

What aggravates the case is the passive attitude on the part of the Jew himself. "Instead of realizing their own position and adopting a rational line of conduct, the Jews appeal to eternal justice."[61] They fail to realize that in order to produce a different effect, the cause must be changed. Loss of self-respect by denial of their identity, obsequious self-effacement and retreat before a hostile opponent, can hardly earn for them the human dignity requisite for acceptance as an equal. The very reliance upon the Messiah has often proved a subterfuge for initiative required to attain self-liberation. The cumulative result is a syndrome of ills, inner and outer forces in collusion, militating against a constructive course of Jewish survival. Delusive too is the mission idea which rationalizes a historical calamity into a theological privilege in defining Jewish dispersion as coveted *noblesse oblige.* So much for Pinsker's diagnosis.

In referring to the Messiah and to the Jewish mission, Pinsker alludes to an issue which for many decades evoked considerable controversy in religious quarters. Obviously, a reinterpretation of the concepts of Messiah and missionhood was required to solicit the cooperation of Orthodox and Reform Jews, respectively, for an activist program of return to the homeland.

The author maintains that Jewry can extricate itself from the quicksand of human degradation by a plan of self-help instead of reliance upon others. This would entail a national revival of concerted effort to achieve unity and independence, parallel in scope to other nations. It would mean having a home, a geographically viable territory which Jews could call their own.

The territorialism of Pinsker was not limited to Palestine. At first he preferred other locations. He failed to appreciate the intricate historical and religious association with the Holy Land, or recognize that it alone could generate within the Jewish heart the power for sacrifice, creativity and perseverence required for the regeneration of the people and reconstruction of the homeland. Motivated, at the outset, by objective, practical and human considerations, he hinted at the possibility of an independent Jewish place of refuge somewhere in America. However, after the appearance of *Auto-Emancipation,* Pinsker yielded to expressed Jewish sentiment for Palestine.

The age was most propitious for such an undertaking, according to the assertion of Pinsker. Other ethnic groups were obtaining their national independence. Mass emigration from Russia—multitudes on the run instead of a nation on the march—could be redirected in part toward a permanent home in an autonomous Jewish country. The first signs of an awakened self-consciousness were already evident, stemming from a disenchantment with the slogans which had failed. World public opinion could now be expected to respond more favorably to Jewish demands for territorial independence. It was incumbent upon the wealthiest and most powerful Jews of the Occident to rush to the aid of the less fortunate in a manner that assured rehabilitation rather than temporary relief provided by unimaginative charity.

Consequently, the call of the hour was for (a) the existing societies of organized Jews in various lands to "convoke a national congress"[62] that would speak in the name of a united people; (b) the national congress to locate a suitable territory and secure it as inalienable national property sufficient for the settlement "in the course of time several million Jews";[63] (c) the formation of a "stock company" to purchase land, reapportion and resell it equitably to prospective colonists, and provide additional funds from profits and charitable collections for destitute immigrants.

To implement the colonization project soundly and efficaciously, Pinsker regarded international recognition as a prerequisite. "The establishment of a Jewish refuge cannot come about without the support of the governments."[64] Furthermore, a large-scale transfer of population is impractical if not impossible. The territory could receive only the annual surplus population from areas of larger Jewish concentration. In addition, the existence of a sovereign Jewish state would profoundly affect the fate of Jews elsewhere in the world. The abnormality of their previous position would disappear, for in their new status as aliens and members of a minority related to a home base, they would invite no exceptional treatment. Simultaneously, the attainment of nationhood would inspire individual self-acceptance and identification in place of humiliating self-abnegation. Yet a miraculous rebirth could not be expected within the span of a few years. The recovery could not be spontaneous. "We must take the first step. Our descendants must follow at a measured and not over-precipitant speed."[65] But the beginning is to be launched immediately. It is 'now or never'.

IV

The strength of Pinsker's message was not in its originality. In many ideas he had been preceded by Hebrew writers. His was the first presentation in a European tongue to reach a large public. His views were timely, and thus became timeless. His analysis of anti-Semitism was original and incisive; the attack upon emancipation, denuding; the insight into the social condition of Jews, penetrating; the appeal for action, eloquent; and the spelling out of a program, practical. The fact that his ambitious plans and dramatic plea were of no great immediate consequence is not the fault of Pinsker. He was the pioneer who pointed the way, and he drew up the blueprints. The movement of *Hibat Zion* placed the mantle of leadership upon his shoulders against his will. He was neither young enough nor strong enough to transform operations into realities. Another fifteen years elapsed before there appeared upon the scene the architect of the movement that paved the road to auto-emancipation.

In the ensuing march of time and events, Pinsker's great little booklet *Auto-Emancipation* continued to pose a number of important premises of lasting relevance. Foremost is the conviction that "humanity and enlightenment alone will not cure the malady of our people," but that Jewish initiative and self-reliance, not only in philanthropy but in the political and cultural domains, will save and secure the nation. Of primary importance, therefore, is not what others do for the Jews, but what Jews do for themselves as a people entitled to its place as one among equals. Implicit in this approach is the claim that the creation of a homeland is not an act of retreat and withdrawal from humanity, but the only logical and dignified co-existence in a world community as it is constituted today and, most likely, will be for some time to come. The cementing of national unity and preservation of corporate entity are predicated upon and conducive to the restoration of human stature, self-acceptance and wholesomeness of personality on the part of the individual as well. Pinsker's thesis suggests that normalizing the national status of

Jewry, and assuring the independence, dignity and security of the State of Israel, may prove the soundest basis for interfaith relations. These are axioms which have been enunciated, reiterated and verified in the Zionist debate of decades. Pinsker made an invaluable contribution by his personal example. For a man beyond sixty years of age to abandon a life-long commitment, and champion with renewed vigor a cause in conflict with his previously held views, requires unusual courage and integrity. History is replete with religious conversions of old and young; but an intellectual re-evaluation, secular in character, leading to a denial of the allegiance of a lifetime, is exceedingly rare.

V

A comparison between Hess and Pinsker is illuminating. The influence of the latter was considerably greater than that of the former. While Hess was a voice calling out in the wilderness, removed from large Jewish centers in his French isolation, Pinsker was a Russian Jew in contact with his people who found fertile ground for his ideas in the immediate environment and received at least vocal endorsement from a movement that had come into being.

But Pinsker's metamorphosis was of more impressive dimensions. The German Jew, who had been totally estranged from Judaism, could make a clean break with the outside world, return to his people and begin anew. In Pinsker's case, there had been many decades spent in dedicated, though misdirected, activity within the Jewish community in a joint venture with others, directed toward the goals of assimilation. His was the painful and tedious task of destroying the old crop and replanting new seed in the same ground.

Hess and Pinsker were complementary to each other. Hess spoke primarily in religious-cultural terms, while Pinsker dealt in political and social realities. Each approach affects the inner constitution of man and his outer deportment. To Hess, Israel was the spiritual citadel of the Jewish heritage; to Pinsker, Israel was the physical refuge for the Jewish people. These were the two parallel currents in the Zionist stream which irrigated the parched soil of national Jewish consciousness throughout the century. These remain the irreducible axioms of Zionist thought and education as they are currently operative in Israel and Jewish communities abroad.

A NATIONAL TONGUE

Eliezer Ben Yehuda

I

A COMMON LANGUAGE is essential to the making of a nation. A few sovereign states, such as Canada, Switzerland, Belgium and India have more than one official tongue; but this is the exception rather than the rule. Each of these countries is sub-divided into administrative areas, generally corresponding to its linguistic divisions. Nevertheless, the language differential often becomes an internal source of friction whenever the status quo is threatened.

The Jews, returning to their homeland, brought with them as many languages as the countries from which they emanated. To these languages they clung, some out of loyalty and others because of necessity. The result was serious confusion which often led to conflict as cities and villages were established, and schools and institutions were founded. To unite a people in its ancestral home without reducing the towering Babel of languages, presented difficulties which appeared insurmountable. It was therefore incumbent upon Zionism to cope with the problem of language in addition to facing the challenges of land, government, society and culture.

In the plethora of problems, ideological and practical, secular and spiritual, the language issue was ignored by the pioneers of Zionist thought, Hess, Pinsker, and even Smolenskin. Theodore Herzl, founder of the Zionist Movement, in his novel *Old-New Land,* takes for granted an existing European medium of communication. Exponents of cultural or spiritual Zionism, while elaborating upon the need for a modern Hebrew literature and Hebrew education in the classics, were oblivious to the importance of *one* national vernacular, usually entertaining every possibility except Hebrew. Throughout the dispersion, two Jewish languages were widely accepted—Yiddish, and to a lesser extent, Ladino. The former, mother tongue of millions of East European Jews, with its flourishing literature, press and theatre, was coming into its own at the turn of the century. Yet, it was derogatorily designated as a jargon by both sophisticated Hebraists in Eastern Europe and the assimilated occidental intelligentsia. Ladino, which did not have the stature of Yiddish, was the Spanish-Hebrew dialect of Mediterranean Jewish communities. Among the residents of Palestine it was fashionable to converse in German, French or Russian. To a less significant extent, English, Polish, Hungarian, Bulgarian, Roumanian, Italian and Arabic were used. Twelve major languages that received the lip-service of a numerically small group assembled in a limited geographical area, plus an equal number of other tongues less frequently heard, could hardly achieve cohesiveness, harmony and integration necessary for the reconstruction of land, economy and society, not to mention the preservation and development of a national culture!

Hebrew, as a spoken language, was therefore a *sine qua non* in the new Israel. This self-evident truth was first recognized by one person, Eliezer Ben Yehuda, who made its realization his life goal, fanatically pursuing it for over forty years. Starting what could be regarded as a one-man revolution, he accomplished his objective with amazing success. In the course of total commitment he turned his personal obsession into a national ideal without which Israel society, as it is now constituted, would be inconceivable if not virtually unattainable. The common bond of modern Hebrew, though a reality today, is still stressed as an ideal of the Jewish renaissance, a valued component of the Zionist synthesis and the Israel intellectual climate. Hebrew was the only tongue that linked all Jewish tribes, regardless of their country of origin. Prior to its rebirth in Israel, Hebrew was not used by any one group as the medium of conversation; but prayers, texts, legal and religious documents and inter-community missives were composed in Hebrew for nearly two thousand years throughout the course of Jewish history, ever since the Jewish people was driven out of its Hebrew home. Moreover, a secular Hebrew literature and press had arisen in Europe during the nineteenth century. The revival of spoken Hebrew, therefore, appeared as a logical and practical necessity as well as a historical requirement. On the debit side it should be recorded that, of the languages previously listed, Hebrew was the only one which was regarded as "dead"—the language of the book rather than of life. It lacked the basic everyday vocabulary and forms of expression necessary for modern usage. To cite one example, the word for "please" was rendered in a cumbersome clause. Though abounding in philosophical and religious terms, Hebrew was poor in essential words for use in the kitchen, market place, factory and playground. Hebrew constructions were antiquated and circumlocutionary. As a holy tongue that had not been profaned in daily life for perhaps thousands of years, it was unsuitable for a fast-thinking, rapid-speaking, sharp-tongued people who were inspired to assume heroic ventures and draw upon untapped energies in the upbuilding of a nation. Obviously, more than preaching was necessary to overcome what appeared to be overwhelming obstacles in the revival of Hebrew. Ben Yehuda accepted the challenge, never resting nor faltering until the job was completed by the end of his life.

II

Born Eliezer Perlman in Lithuania in 1858, Ben Yehuda received the customary religious instruction. At the age of twelve, he was sent away from home for advanced studies in a school where he came under the influence of a teacher who secretly initiated him in the study of Hebrew grammar, and introduced him to those books of the Bible which were not included in the traditional curriculum. These were frowned upon as digressions that interfered with the study of Talmud. Transferred to another school, he had the good fortune to be welcomed into a family of culture and means; and there he met his future wife who tutored him in preparation for the entrance examinations of a Russian high school. He continued with his general schooling and, breaking with his religious upbringing, identified himself with the socialist movement.

The Russian-Turkish war of 1877-8, which led to independence for the Balkan nationalities, suggested to him the possibility of Jewish statehood in Palestine. At about the same time, he came upon George Eliot's novel *Daniel Deronda* which had a profound influence upon him because of its espousal of the return of Jews to their ancestral homeland. He went to Paris to study medicine, planning to be a physician in Palestine. Stricken with tuberculosis, he was hospitalized and compelled to retire for a rest cure in Algiers. Finally, in 1881, at the age of twenty-three, he set out with his bride for Palestine. Living, according to his doctors, on "borrowed time," he spent the next forty-one years in Jerusalem (with occasional trips abroad in conjunction with his work), teaching, editing, writing and engaging in many controversies until his passing, in 1922, at the age of sixty-four.

While still in Paris young Perlman, who had adopted the Hebrew name of Ben Yehuda, published in 1879 an essay entitled "A Weighty Question." It appeared in Smolenskin's *Hashahar* in Vienna, after being rejected by another Hebrew periodical. Ben Yehuda's literary debut was an assault upon assimilation and pursued a line of attack similar to that of Smolenskin. But he was a step ahead of the master in urging a return to the homeland, prior to the latter's conversion to the cause. He traced the contemporary rise of European nationalism and came to the conclusion that

> . . . we Hebrews have the same right; for why should our lot be inferior to that of other nations? . . . Why should we be robbed of the hope to return to a national life in our devastated land which mourns for her children who have been driven off to distant lands some two thousand years before?[66]

The same article contained the germ of the idea which became the fixation of a lifetime:

> Why do some of our people claim that we are not qualified for national life since we do not speak one language? . . . We do have a language in which we can write down all of our thoughts, and we can speak it too if we should so desire.[67]

The essay, appearing before the crucial year of 1881, was considered radical even by the editor. He expressed his reservations; but later on, convinced by the tragic events of the times, he accepted Ben Yehuda's reasoning. Against the "spiritual nationalism" which Smolenskin had derived from his own philosophy of Judaism, Ben Yehuda postulated a political nationalism sparked by the European national upsurge he was witnessing. Smolenskin saw the need for a deepened sense of united peoplehood among the far-flung remnants, to assure survival in the diaspora. Ben Yehuda found this emphasis necessary but inadequate, unless followed by a return to Palestine. The disease of assimilation, Ben Yahuda maintained, had not only infected western Jews enamoured of the lure of enlightenment; it had also felled eastern Jews who were leaving the ghetto. Ultimate disintegration was natural and logical as long as religion was losing its medieval hold. A political center of gravity, which also serves as a cultural stronghold, is a historical imperative in light of the exigencies of the age.

Ben Yehuda reaffirmed his faith in the national redemption of Israel and the revival of Hebrew by elaborating upon his first call with further appeals. National redemption of Israel and the revival of Hebrew are inseparable from each other. The latter is the logical complement of the former and unattainable without it.

> We shall not be able to revive the Hebrew language except in the land where a majority of the inhabitants are Hebrews. Let us, therefore, increase the number of Jews in our desolate land, and return the remnant of our people to the soil of their ancestors. Let us restore the nation to life, and its language shall live again.[68]

Unlike his predecessors and contemporaries, Ben Yehuda's nationalism was secular. He took the extreme view of linguistic territorial nationalism independent of spiritual values. In combining territory and language, he also rejected a Hebrew language dissociated from the nation restored to its land. "If I had not believed in the redemption of the Jews, I would have cast away Hebrew as a useless thing."[69] Smolenskin's literary Hebraism, devoid of the normal forms of nationalism, appeared quite inconsistent to Ben Yehuda. Operating within a secular nationalistic frame of reference, he concluded that "Judaism shall be Hebrew Palestinian, or it shall not be at all."[70] He denied the possibility of survival in the lands of dispersion, being the first in the camp of the "negators of exile", in the great Zionist debate which was waged on this issue for over half a century. The "negators" denied any hope for Jewish survival outside Israel, even if the threat of anti-Semitism be mitigated or eliminated, for Jewishness could not hold its own against the competition of the majority culture. Consequently, attempts to transmit the Hebrew language outside of Palestine were noble but ineffective without the natural base in Palestine. Ben Yehuda, to avoid any misrepresentation, explicitly defines the new nationalism in unequivocal terms:

> Three things are inscribed in fiery letters on the national banner: land, a national language, and a national education. To deny one of them is to negate the essence of nationalism.[71]

The impassioned idealist was a man of action who translated ideas into deeds by beginning with himself. Once he was converted to Zionism, he immigrated to Palestine and settled in Jerusalem, a community most inhospitable to a young man molded by a European university. The local Jewish population was made up of a disproportionately large number of older people from all parts of the world who had come here to await eventual burial in the Holy Land—a hallowed custom of ages among pious Jews. They subsisted as beneficiaries of the traditional charity system while they spent their time in study and prayer without engaging in any form of gainful employment. The funds were provided by *Haluka* ("distribution") based on small but world-wide charity collections gathered by various Jewish agencies for the support of the people of their respective countries residing in the "holy cities" of Jerusalem, Safed, Hebron and Tiberias.

The members of this elderly community were fanatically devoted to the minutiae of ritual and custom, and tightly insulated against the slightest manifestation of modernism. Ben Yehuda brazenly took upon himself the three-fold revolution of cultivating spoken Hebrew, propagandizing Zionist principles and advocating a productive pattern of existence in place of what he regarded as a parasitic way of life.

Ben Yehuda's triumphs and defeats reflect more than the biographical data of one person. The particulars of his life are part of the national saga of a generation. He influenced by personal example. Details of his public battles and private struggles are interwoven with the fabric of Israel to an extent rarely if ever approximated by any individual who came after him. Of the twelve spiritual architects of Israel presented in this book, he alone settled in Palestine in his youth (at the age of twenty-three) and continued in total dedication, both of himself and his family to the cause he espoused. The colorful, romantic events of his heroic life, interrelated as they were with the epic story of the rebirth of a people, have captured the imagination of a Christian writer whose biography, in English, of Ben Yehuda still enjoys considerable popularity.[72]

III

Ben Yehuda's call for a return to the land of Israel and the revival of the Hebrew language took the Jewish public by surprise, coming as it did three years before Pinsker's epochal *Auto-Emancipation,* and two years before the Russian pogroms of 1881. His own spiritual confreres had little faith in the success of his mission.

> When Smolenskin saw that his pupil intended to rebuild Zion's ruins with his own hands, he hastened to warn him against it, comparing his desire "to that of a man attempting to build a tower on the roof before erecting the house. . . . And if your intention is to clear the way for the coming of the Messiah, both the believers and the enlightened shall rise up against you."[73]

But the pupil took no heed.

Soon after he adopted a Hebrew surname, Ben Yehuda began his campaign for Hebrew by insisting upon its exclusive use in his own home, though his wife was completely ignorant of the language. With unrelenting stubbornness he persisted in his course, addressing his infant son only in Hebrew, thereby preventing the child from communicating with playmates. He influenced other intellectuals to form the first Hebrew-speaking club. As a teacher in the French-speaking *Alliance* school in Jerusalem, he introduced the method of teaching "Hebrew in Hebrew" as a natural living tongue. Gradually his influence spread to other schools. He edited a periodical, *Hatzvi,* ("The Deer"—a Biblical reference to the Holy Land) and made it a champion for the revival of Hebrew. He declared war on the German-Jewish sponsored schools that refused to adopt Hebrew, thereby jeopardizing the subsidies he received for his literary activity.

The path was a thorny one. The exclusive use in his own home of a language no one else spoke, retarded the speech development of his own son who was relatively inarticulate at an age when most children are able to express themselves. The Orthodox opposed Ben Yehuda on the grounds that a holy tongue should not be desecrated in kitchen and bathroom parlance. The modern elements scoffed at the poverty of expression in everyday speech, and the limitations of Hebrew in the academic disciplines. Officials of European Jewish agencies operating in Palestine regarded his efforts as a threat to the French, German and English cultures they were separately propagating. The leading Hebrew writers had little faith in the undertaking. Zionist leaders merely tolerated his obsession. He suffered excommunication by the Rabbinate, imprisonment by the Turks, scorn by acquaintances. When his wife died she was refused burial rites. His children were subjected to ridicule and hostility. Stronger men would have admitted defeat. Unswerving in his loyalty and zeal, he remained the dauntless missionary, accepting temporary defeat with equanimity.

In time, Hebrew teachers and the young pioneers who were stirred by his calls for action responded favorably to the linguistic challenge, and rallied behind his banner. Ben Yehuda built the first Hebrew home; his wife was the first Hebrew mother; his son was the first Hebrew-speaking child in centuries. Soon there were others who followed his example. Eventually, after the first World War, Hebrew as a living tongue infiltrated Jewish schools in Europe and America.

After his wife's death, her younger sister arrived from Russia to take her place by his side, joining wholeheartedly in the dedication to her newly acquired tongue, and sharing Ben Yehuda's tribulations for over thirty years.

IV

To breathe life into the Hebrew language, Ben Yehuda had to become the scholar in addition to the soldier and idealist.

> The revival of the Hebrew language in Palestine created the need for new words and expressions, names for objects and concepts unknown in ancient times, scientific terms and definitions, forms of expression for modern thought. Ben Yehuda involuntarily became the linguist, the great innovator in the field of Hebrew philology.[74]

This was codified in his life work, *The Complete Hebrew Dictionary*. Of the sixteen volumes which he prepared, he saw five in print and eleven were published posthumously. The last volume appeared at the end of the nineteen-fifties.

The monumental compilation by Ben Yehuda is more than a dictionary. It includes a thesaurus, grammatical, philological and etymological studies, as well as numerous neologisms of his own creation. He undertook the task of gathering all the words of a three-thousand-year-old literature which was diffused over many lands, in order to modernize an ancient tongue and create a vocabulary for daily and scientific usage. To achieve this he laboriously searched in person the libraries of Europe and America, communicated with scholars all over the world, and examined countless books, manuscripts and documents, rediscovering words, borrowing terms, adapting forms and coining new words in accordance with the linguistic requirements of modern Hebrew. Most of his innovations, though not all, were eventually accepted. He, too, was the one who decided in favor of the Sfardi (Spanish and Levantine) pronunciation of Hebrew, in place of the Ashkenazi dialect in vogue among the majority of Jews in the world in his day, and still used in most synagogues in America and Europe.

Ben Yehuda remained an unswerving nationalist with a single-minded dedication. He relegated religious, social and economic considerations to less important positions below that of the Hebrew language. During his diversified career he often aligned himself with anti-religious forces, joined Herzl in the territorialist deviation to Uganda for a temporary haven of refuge, and lashed out mercilessly against all distractions from the nationalist aim. With fantastic and fanatic zeal he championed the cause of Hebrew until he was privileged to witness its recognition by the British Mandatory regime in Palestine as an official language, along with Arabic and English.

> His personality fused two seemingly contradictory characteristics: scholarly research in withered folios, and the war-like spirit of a man of action; the moderation of an erudite man and the fiery temperament of a political combatant. . . . An ancient spark ignited in his heart became a burning flame illuminating the path of many exiles to the one and only land.[75]

Ben Yehuda's English biographer concludes his work with this succinct statement of fact:

> When Ben Yehuda started work on his dream, Hebrew was only a liturgical medium, as dead as ancient Latin. . . . By the time he made his last trip up the Mount of Olives, a new and vibrant Hebrew was being spoken by a new and vibrant race of Jews.[76]

It is interesting to note that in the Irish Free State a sovereign government, with all the means of support and control at its disposal, ruling an independent nation on its own soil, has had little success in reviving the indigenous national Gaelic tongue. What a modern state failed to accomplish with all its machinery of government, a frail, tubercular man with little assistance from anyone except some young enthusiasts, achieved in his own lifetime, adding one more miracle to the seven wonders of the world.

Ben Yehuda's first challenging and fructifying ideas on nationalism are over-shadowed by the crowning Herculian effort which established him for posterity as the Father of the Modern Hebrew Language. Hebrew, as we know it today, is alive because Ben Yehuda lived.

BLUEPRINTS OF A STATE

Theodor Herzl

I

MORE THAN any other individual, Theodor Herzl influenced the course of contemporary Jewish history by founding the movement which set out to establish the Jewish State in Palestine. In historical perspective, Herzl emerges as the greatest Jew in centuries; the impact of his life and work is unique and lasting. Meteor-like, he streaked across the darkened Jewish skies, leaving a trail of light in his path, and was consumed by the momentum of his course. In less than a decade of service to his people, in a life prematurely ended at the age of forty-four, he transformed the face of Jewry, enabling it to begin a new chapter of heroic revival. He launched an era which, within half a century thereafter, changed a two thousand year old dream into a reality—the reality of the State of Israel.

Theodor Herzl was born in 1860 in Budapest into a typically "emancipated" Jewish middle-class family which was steeped in German culture. His early education at a school maintained by the sophisticated segment of the Jewish community included but a minimum of Jewish training. When he was eighteen his family moved to Vienna where Herzl prepared for the degree of Doctor of Laws. After one year of practice he abandoned law for a literary career as a playwright and feuilletonist. He became associated with a leading Vienna newspaper, and as its Paris correspondent attended the Dreyfus trial. The trial involved a Jewish captain of the French army who had been falsely accused of treason. The case, which became a *cause celebre,* was eventually exposed as an attempt to find a Jewish scapegoat for treachery which had occurred within the French General Staff.

The Dreyfus trial rocked Europe and shocked Herzl. In earlier years, while he was a student and during his journalistic career, he had witnessed the rise of racial anti-Semitism as an organized, aggressive force that was enjoying the support of both the ignorant and the educated in the rising national movements. In school, he had experienced anti-Jewish hostility among the students. In adult life, he was confronted with the difficulty of pursuing a successful law career in the midst of increasing discrimination. He came to realize that many Jewish professionals were consciously becoming alienated from their religion and people, hoping for the ultimate elimination of prejudice by the liberating powers of a new age destined to dawn on Europe. It was then that Herzl himself entertained the idea that mass conversion was an escape from the ills of bigotry. An entry in his diary reads: "At first the Jewish problem hurt me sorely. Perhaps there was a time when I would gladly have escaped into Christianity—anywhere."[77]

But the Dreyfus Affair was the turning point in his life. It brought into bold the defenselessness of the Jew, making him a vulnerable target even in an enlightened age in the most advanced capital of Europe. Some years afterward Herzl wrote:

> The Dreyfus case embodies more than a judicial error; it embodies a desire of the vast majority of the French to condemn all Jews in this one Jew. . . . Death to the Jews! howled the mob. . . . Where? In France: republican, modern, civilized France, a hundred years after the Declaration of the Rights of Man![78]

The episode started a train of thought with new insights into the nature of anti-Semitism, undermining Herzl's previous convictions:

> Until that time most of us believed that the solution to the Jewish question was to be patiently waited for as part of the general development of mankind.[79]

It then flashed upon him that this was too long a period to wait. . . . In the throes of emotional reaction to the dramatic miscarriage of justice in Paris, he composed *The Jewish State,* ushering in the dawn of political Zionism. It was published in 1896.

In the following year, Herzl called together in Basle representatives of Jewish groups from the world-over for the historic sessions of the First Zionist Congress which formulated the official Zionist program and set up the movement bearing its name. He remained its leader through the stormy years of subsequent Congresses, until his untimely passing in 1904.

Herzl's influence on the contemporary scene emanated from two sources: the book he authored, and the movement he organized and led. Unlike his precursors, he was a man of action whose leadership captured the imagination of the masses, galvanizing them into unprecedented spirited activity.

II

In Herzl's pre-Zionist days the Jewish Problem possessed his thoughts. A play of his entitled *The New Ghetto* depicted the tragedy of the emancipated Jew admitted into the modern world but not accepted by it. He offered the solution in a little book of less than one hundred pages, *The Jewish State,* recognized as one of the great books that forged Jewish destiny through the ages. He was not aware of Pinsker's pamphlet, as he later testified, for had he read the former's *Auto-Emancipation,* he never would have written his own book.

In *The Jewish State* Herzl presents both a concise exposition of the grievous Jewish question and an answer formulated in a detailed blueprint. He sums up his thesis in these words:

> Let the sovereignty be granted us over a portion of the globe, large enough to satisfy the rightful requirements of a nation; the rest we shall manage for ourselves.[80]

"The Jewish question still exists," he states in the introduction. Eventually humanity may rise to greater heights of charity and understanding, and bring an end to Jewish suffering. But this is too far distant, "beyond our day, beyond the days of our children, of our grandchildren and our great-grandchildren."[81] He dissects anti-Semitism in all its negative components, pointing beyond the official religious bias to its social, economic and psychological motives. Political emancipation, he claims, which removed the legal barriers against Jews, has caused additional friction, since liberated men entering the professions and free business ventures present the threat of economic competition. It is not feasible to withdraw equal rights nor can the Jewish group be singled out for effective curtailment of commercial enterprise since this would prove injurious to the general economic structure; hence anti-Semitism becomes a seething infection, often reaching in its frustration to a dangerous point of eruption. Thus there is formed a vicious circle wherein Jews, in desperation, identify themselves with revolutionary causes or strive successfully toward economic ascendency to escape middle-class pressure and prejudice. In both instances, unfortunately, the wells of hostility continue to be replenished.[82]

Herzl argued that assimilation, even if possible, is not a solution—a fact amply demonstrated in the experiences of his own generation. Only total fusion through intermarriage can eventually eliminate the problem; but as long as there is some Jewish identification there will be anti-Jewish reactions. Jews are thus "one people" bound together by a common destiny in a hostile world.

The answer lies in the creation of a Jewish State. The first step is to organize a "Society of Jews" as the political representative of the Jewish people, and to launch the "Jewish Company" as its financial and executive agent to administer mass colonization in a new territory. Through its newly formed authorized leadership, organized Jewry will solicit from some great power sovereignty over "a portion of the globe". Such representation, of course, will be made only in behalf of Jews affiliated with the Society.

> Those Jews who agree with our idea of a State will attach themselves to the Society, which will thereby be authorized to confer and treat with Governments in the name of our people. The Society will thus be acknowledged in its relations with Governments as a State-creating power.[83]

For the territory to be selected, Herzl's choice was Palestine or Argentina, the latter then being the seat of extensive

Jewish colonization, financed by the Paris philanthropist, Baron de Hirsch. Herzl had expressed a preference for the former, though not an exclusive one. The unfolding plan of statehood outlined liquidation of property, transportation of immigrants, and resettlement in the new land. Advanced managerial methods and technological discoveries were to be utilized in the rehabilitation of the people. The "seven hour day" was to be the regular working day of the new society to be established on economically sound and socially progressive principles conducive to maximum human benefit. There was further elaboration of social welfare policies, organization of commerce to eliminate unsavory or unsound financial speculation, planned housing, industrial promotion and methods of financing the initial enterprise. Capital was to be raised through bank loans and by public subscription.[84] The plan further called for immigration regulated by the Society, transplanting existing communities *in toto* to enable them to preserve their social and cultural traditions. He predicted that "those who are now desperate will go first, after them the poor; next the prosperous, and last of all, the wealthy."[85]

"The idea of a Jewish State, though not new," Herzl asserted, was never as feasible as at present. "A hundred— or even fifty years ago it would have been nothing more than a dream. Today it may become a reality."[86] Scientific progress will make possible a project on such a large scale.

In *Old-New Land,* a later book of fiction depicting the Jewish Utopia, Herzl suggests that the existence of an independent state would relieve as well those who choose to remain behind. It would be possible for them to sever their ties with the Jewish people without regret or reproach, once Jewish political sovereignty is a fact:[87]

> Jews who wish to assimilate with other peoples now felt free to do so openly, without cowardice or deception. There were also some who wished to adopt the majority religion, and these could now do so without being suspected of snobbery or careerism, for it was no longer to one's advantage to abandon Judaism.[88]

The salutary effects would begin immediately without having to wait for the attainment of statehood. "If we only begin to carry out our plans, anti-Semitism would stop for once and forever."[89] The new role of the Jew would elicit respect from all. The citizen of the Jewish State, residing in security and freedom, would inevitably prove a better human being, elevated and rehabilitated by the therapeutic powers of the new society, which was to be founded on the noblest ideals of mankind and was to develop within the framework of the most advanced scientific knowledge of the age. Herzl's manifesto concludes in a crescendo of the theme:

> And what glory awaits those who fight unselfishly for the cause!
>
> Therefore I believe that a wondrous generation of Jews will spring into existence. The Maccabeans will rise again.
>
> . . . The Jews who wish for a State will have it.
>
> We shall live at last as free men on our own soil, and die peacefully in our own homes.
>
> The world will be freed by our liberty, enriched by our wealth, magnified by our greatness.
>
> And whatever we attempt there to accomplish for our own welfare, will react powerfully and beneficially for the good of humanity.[90]

The daring vision of the Jewish State is continued in the aforementioned utopian dream of *Old-New Land,* published in 1902. Twenty years afterwards the author revisits the Jewish homeland (by now definitely located in Palestine without the equivocation of his earlier work) and finds a reconstituted model commonwealth,

> where the intellectual proletariat of Central Europe would exercise their skill in law, medicine, journalism, administration, engineering, architecture, art, music, and philosophy for the upbuilding and progress of the land, and the proletarian masses of Eastern Europe drop their peddlers' packs to become straight-backed, sun-bronzed peasants and artisans. Then the Jew, degraded to less than man's estate by anti-Semitism, would regain the full stature of manhood on his own soil . . .[91]

The successful experiment is an example to mankind. One of the heroes of the novel asserts that the Jewish people is the logical choice to lead in industrial and social pioneering:

> "Only we Jews could have done it," replied David calmly . . . "We only were in a position to create this new society, this new center of civilization here."[92]

Both Herzl's vision and plan were structured on a premise of international import. Insisting that the Jewish problem is one of national dimension for both Jews and Gentiles, and not merely religious or social, Herzl urged that it "be raised to political world rank." Governments, out of a sense of humanitarian duty and enlightened self-interest, should cooperate in bringing this about.

It was expected that such a plan would arouse, in Herzl's own words, "a mighty cry of agreement in every place where Jews suffer."

> The cry was all the mightier because the Jewish masses had never expected to hear such a voice from such a quarter—from a German assimilationist writer and journalist, from

> one without a Zionist past, almost without a Jewish one. And this was a mighty voice . . . a triumphant bugle call—deep and vibrant, because it expressed the liberation of the man himself.[93]

More than half a century later, Chaim Weizmann, first president of Israel, reminisces on the reaction to *The Jewish States*:

> The effect produced was profound. Not the ideas, but the personality which stood behind them appealed to us. Here was daring, clarity and energy. The very fact that this Westerner came to us unencumbered by our own preconceptions had its appeal.[94]

Student groups and leading western Jewish intellectuals, such as the French social philosopher Max Nordau and the English novelist Israel Zangwill, were won over to the cause. The magnetic personality of Herzl also attracted disciples among non-Jews.

Though preceded by Hess and Pinsker, Herzl's idea was a revelation to some and an apostasy to others. His predecessors had discussed anti-Semitism and suggested an autonomous State as the remedy. But they were unknown to Herzl's contemporaries. Besides, his carefully spelled out plan for organization and program of actual implementation to achieve the goal was novel and attractive. It immediately created "among a small but immensely influential group of Western Jews, a new Jewish consciousness."[95]

III

It soon became evident to Herzl himself that he could not adhere to the intention initially stated in the preface to *The Jewish State*. "I feel that with the publication of this pamphlet, my task is done."[96] He set out fervently and feverishly to drive toward the goal. He conceded to public sentiment by shifting from territorialism generally, to Zionism specifically. "When I began, I thought only of a Jewish State. But now I have become a Lover of Zion. In my eyes there is no other solution to the great national problem known as the Jewish Question, except the Land of Israel."[97] In 1897 he called together the first Zionist Congress as the Society of Jews designated in the original plan. The opening address contained these memorable words: "We want to lay the foundations of the edifice which is one day to house the Jewish people."[98] Having assembled around him recognized Jewish dignitaries, and prepared with the pageantry necessary for an auspicious beginning, he struck a high pitch of enthusiasm and solemnity in the formal inauguration of Zionism as a political movement. The Congress kindled the spirit and set the stage for great things to come.

The following years were tense with concentrated activity on the international arena. He conferred with the Kaiser, Pope and Sultan, as well as the British, Austrian, Roumanian and Russian ministers, and sought the aid of Jewish philanthropists. His missions took him to all the capitals of Europe and to Palestine. In Russia, Jewish crowds welcomed him as "King of the Jews."

As far as immediate results were concerned, there were none, since the coveted "charter" for Palestine was not offered during his lifetime. Counting on the potential support of Jewish financiers, he contemplated bartering financial backing for the bankrupt Sultan government, in exchange for a "charter". This he did not succeed in attaining. However, international recognition of the Zionist movement was granted in 1903 by the British offer of Uganda in East Africa as a Jewish haven of refuge under

Zionist auspices. Discussion of this proposal inspired the most dramatic moment and painful schism at a Zionist Congress, when the dissenters accused Herzl and his followers of treason to the Zionist ideal. With a sense of immediacy sparked by the Kishinev pogrom of 1903, Herzl was amenable to any territorial opportunity for colonization and sovereignty, an expedient departure which the loyal followers of Zion were unwilling to accept. Herzl died the following year.

IV

During the eight years of Herzl's dynamic leadership, the instrumentalities of Zionism were forged. A permanent world representative body was established for the far-flung communities of Jewry; an anthem, flag and statement of aims adopted; a bank for colonization formed; and, to purchase land in Palestine, the Jewish National Fund was organized. The Zionist Congress became a permanent institution, meeting first annually and then biennially as the united Jewish tribune speaking to the nations of the world. The Congress continues to reconvene to the present day. After the establishment of the state in 1948, sessions have been held in Jerusalem with the participation of elected delegates from all over the world, Russia and its satellites excepted. In the short period of a few years, Zionism emerged from humble beginnings and sporadic strivings to an organized vital force operating in behalf of the Jewish people on the international scene. At the end of the World War I, the charter goal was realized with the Balfour Declaration of the British Government on the "establishment of a Jewish national home in Palestine". The mandate of the League of Nations gave international recognition to the Basle program, formally accepting that which Herzl had striven so vigorously to attain, and entrusting the British Government with its implementation.

Herzl was wrong in many respects. Remote from the traditional way of life, he failed at first to appreciate sufficiently the importance of religious and cultural ethnic values in the reconstructed Jewish society of the future. Some of his accepted notions, such as the desirability of dueling, were quite alien to the Jewish spirit. Revival of Hebrew was not in his plan. His sanction of assimilation and conversion for Jews dissociating themselves from the new state was, to say the least, unwarranted. Herzl's real contribution was not in the originality of his thought, but in the inspiration of his personality. He reawakened the cherished ancient yearning, spurring on its adherents to the vindication of the hallowed faith of national redemption.

> Herzl was the first—and herein lies his historic greatness—who was able to breathe a new spirit, the will to act, into the faith and nostalgia of the Jewish people yearning to be revived. . . . He transformed the Jewish people for the first time since its Exile into a political force, a fighting creative force . . . capable of reshaping its historic destiny by its own will and exertions.[99]

Such is the evaluation of David Ben Gurion, first premier of Israel.

Herzl was a visionary who strove to convert the Messianic hope into a political reality. He raised the banner of the Jewish State, summoning behind it millions to whom the concept was a cherished wish beyond realization, a prayer encased within the heart, concealed in the Hebrew tongue He uttered the ineffable with daring and forthrightness, describing, demanding, and striving toward its earthly translation. When he first mentioned the Jewish State he was considered mentally deranged. After his death he was regarded as the prophet who prepared for its coming. Herzl's motto, "If you will it, it is no mere legend," became the slogan of two generations who marched on to a new life in the promised land. It is most fitting that Theodor Herzl is the only personage mentioned in that historic document of 1948—Israel's Declaration of Independence.

For the present generation of youth, the first in independent Israel, Herzl is more than an influence. He is the hero of Jewish history whose inspiration and dedication turned a dream into a fact, creating a halo of legendary romance about the life of a person who might be considered almost a contemporary.

Herzl's vision (and therein lies his appeal) was national resurrection in a messianic setting. A few months before his demise, addressing himself to youth, he emphasized that Zionism "as I understand it, contains not only the striving for a legally assured homeland for our people, but also the striving for moral and spiritual perfection".[100] The ideal of individual fulfillment was a factor in the Zionist formula. Therefore it could mean so much in personal terms, uplifting, fulfilling, and reinforcing. "Zionism was the Sabbath of my life," he could admit at the end, in spite of the frustrations and disappointments which studded his path. The sense of mission which inspired his efforts, provided an example for those who have identified themselves with the cause of Zion from its inception to the present day.

> Viewing the whole period in perspective from the vantage point of our day, it may be confidently asserted that never in modern times has a prophet arisen among his people who saw more clearly or endeavoured more nobly to guide his people along the road of honor and security.
>
> It has been his task to overcome the inertia of centuries and set his people into motion. Deliberately and with per-

> sistence, he has striven to dispel the mood of helplessness and dull acquiescence in their fate, and breathe into them a new spirit of self-confidence and the will to achieve. . . . In a remarkable passage of his diary written at the close of the First Congress, he said: "At Basle I founded the Jewish State. If I were to say this today, I would be met by universal laughter. In five years, perhaps, and certainly in fifty, everyone will see it."[101]

He was only one year off in his prediction.

A SPIRITUAL CENTER

Ahad Ha'am

I

Ahad Ha'am may be regarded as the central figure in modern Jewish thought who exerted the greatest influence on Zionist ideology from its early stages to the present day. Periodically expounding his views on contemporary events and issues, he became the leading intellectual authority in the Jewish debate of the twentieth century, affecting social theory, literary standards, educational goals and emerging spiritual concepts. Not only modern Israel but the religious movements in American Jewry owe much to his clarity, incisiveness and originality in defining the essence of Judaism and the problems of Jews. In the impact of his creative thinking he can be compared to the American, John Dewey, though his collected essays comprise but four modest volumes. Like Dewey, he borrowed considerably from his immediate predecessors and was instrumental in the development of a climate of opinion conducive to an all-pervading intellectual reconstruction of society in a changed environment. Like Dewey, he also stimulated far-reaching controversy in various disciplines and was subject to much misrepresentation.

Ahad Ha'am, "One of the People" (the assumed byline of his first essay in 1889 which became his *nomme de plume* for the rest of his life), was born Asher Ginzberg in Ukraine in the year 1865. His home environment, that of a scholarly merchant family, provided opportunity for growth in an atmosphere of study within Jewish tradition, to the exclusion of secular knowledge proscribed in pious quarters. In the seclusion and set pattern of small town life (a wife was chosen for him when he was sixteen years old) Ginzberg devoted himself to his books and secretly delved into foreign languages, classics, philosophy and science. At home and abroad he made a number of unsuccessful attempts to acquire a formal university education. At one time he even left his family to enroll in the University of Vienna, but he soon returned home. As an autodidact he attained comprehensive knowledge of impressive proportions. This pursuit of academic interests is not unrelated to his later emphasis on intellectual and cultural values, as crystallized in his Zionist philosophy.

Ahad Ha'am's creative years were spent in the cities of Odessa and London. In the first location he appeared as the reassessor of pre-Herzlian Zionism, represented by the Russian *Hibat Zion,* where he served in the unofficial though recognized role of spiritual guide for its esoteric circle of altruistic elite named *B'nai Moshe* ("sons of Moses"). The secret society comprised an idealistic group of men dedicated to the cause of Jewish national revival in accordance with Ahad Ha'am's views. Existing for eight years, it included and influenced Russian Jewish personalities who subsequently stood at the helm of the Zionist and Hebrew creative enterprise. On a number of occasions during this period he also visited Palestine, returning with critical but constructive insights. He continued to publicize and develop his ideas through Hebrew periodicals and soon founded and edited his own monthly, *Hashiloah,* which has been regarded as the most important Hebrew publication of the century. Educational and literary ventures, such as the organization of a modern Hebrew school in Jaffa, Palestine, and various Zionist forums in Russia and abroad benefited from his cooperation and leadership.

In 1907, he began the London chapter of his life. He resided there as an official of a tea company, a position which brought him into close contact with personalities such as Chaim Weizmann, the most important figure on the Zionist political scene after Herzl. His influence upon them was direct and profound. In 1922 he moved to Tel Aviv, and died there in 1927 at the age of seventy.

II

Ahad Ha'am's philosophy centered around three categories: Jewish Religion, Jewish People and the Jewish Homeland. These are based on an interpretation of the uniqueness of Judaism, a theory of national survival as a minority in an alien world, and a formulation of Zionism as the solution to the Jewish problem. Together they spell out a *Weltanschauung* of individual, national and universal human values. Ahad Ha'am's theories have a practical application for contemporary Jewish thought and education in Israel and Jewish communities abroad.

Ahad Ha'am accepted the basic religious tenets of Judaism without their theological foundations. To the secular Jew, unfettered by the intellectual and practical discipline of supernatural religion and yet unwilling to cast his moorings in strange waters, a synthesis of traditional values and modern concepts was most welcome. Two alternatives at harmonizing the heritage with modernism had been advocated in the nineteenth century. German Reform struck at the very heart of Judaism by seeking to change radically the Jewish religion; Russian *Haskala* directed itself to the surface by attempting to re-educate Jews in European culture and taste. Recognizing the latter as a matter of course rather than an ideal, Ginzberg approached the spiritual heritage of his people with the criterion of intellectual validity in place of social expediency. The result was a clearer demarcation of Jewish and Christian domains and a renewed emphasis upon the uniqueness of Judaism in its ethical superiority, as evidenced by its past and present performances.

Ahad Ha'am maintained that the Jewish creative genius expressed itself through ethical insight originating with the Prophets, pervading and enobling Jewish experience throughout history. This was manifested in *a total commitment to absolute justice,* uncompromising, indivisible, ubiquitous and specific. The absolute morality of the prophets became meaningful by their particular application in every situation rather than by pious generalization. This is the unique and, regretfully, still the private domain of Judaism. Moses exemplified it; the prophets enunciated it; the Jewish people translated it into a pattern of behavior. The Hebrew creative spirit expressed it in literature. The modern Jew, by intellectual identification with his people, can approximate it without the theological trappings of classical Judaism.

> The fundamental idea of the Hebrew Prophets was the universal dominion of absolute justice. In Heaven it rules through the eternally Righteous, "who holds in His right hand the attribute of judgment," and righteously judges

> all His creatures; and on earth through man, on whom, created in God's image, lies the duty of cherishing the attribute of his Maker, and helping Him, to the best of his meagre power, to guide His world in the path of Righteousness. . . .
>
> Rightousness for them is beauty, it is goodness, wisdom, truth; without it all these are naught.[102]

This is the "national spirit" of the Jewish people which reveals itself both in ethnic culture and in standards of morality. In contrast to Christianity, the ethics of Judaism are based upon justice rather than love—the former, an objective criterion and, therefore, ultimately more conducive to human welfare. Similarly, Ahad Ha'am contends that the Biblical injunction against graven images seeks to avoid representing the ideal (deity) in finite and perceptible forms which make it dependent on specific transient human terms—a moral detraction as well as a theological one:

> If the heathen of the old story, who wished to learn the whole of the Torah while he stood on one foot, had come to me, my reply would have been: " 'Thou shalt not make unto thee any graven image of any likeness,'—that is the whole Torah, and the rest is commentary." What essentially distinguishes Judaism from other religions is its absolute determination to make the religious and moral consciousness independent of any definite human form, and to attach it without any mediating term to an abstract incorporeal ideal.[103]

Thus, Jewish ethics remain absolute yet applicable, idealistic while practical. The commitment is total, yet tangible. This is Jewish experience. Therefore, it spells out Jewish destiny, giving content and direction to national aspirations. To Ahad Ha'am this ethical imperative represented the first attribute of Judaism.

Ahad Ha'am identified a second major attribute of the Jewish religion—its *corporate* character. Fulfillment is gained through the group or nation, in *this* world and not in the hereafter. In the Torah the individual's reward is in the general welfare, and his punishment is in national calamity. Such was the religious promise as long as Israel was a nation on its own land. It was only after the loss of national independence and the dispersion of the people that personal reward and punishment in the hereafter emerged in the religious consciousness:

> . . . Judaism conceives its aim not as the salvation of the individual, but as the well-being and perfection of a group, of the Jewish people and ultimately of the whole human race. . . . The aim is always defined in terms of a collectivity. . . . Judaism had . . . no clear ideal of personal immortality or of reward and punishment after death. The religious and moral inspiration of the Prophets and their disciples was derived . . . from the conviction of their belonging to "the chosen people" which had . . . a divine call to make its national life the embodiment of the highest form of religion and morality. Even in later times . . . the highest aims of Judaism still remained a collective aim.[104]

It follows that the revival of nationalism and the identification of the individual with the destiny of his people is in harmony with original religious tenets. The test of Zionism is to restore the collective consciousness at the expense of unbridled individualism. Zionism is more than a political platform; it is a spiritual credo. A prerequisite is psychological reconditioning in equating personal needs with national goals. This was a latent but unconscious factor in the Jewish psyche for millenia. It must be sufficiently reinforced to generate the added power required to cope with the increasing challenges of contemporary times.

The will of national survival never has been and never should become an unchecked force operating independently within the consciousness of the Jewish people. It is rooted in Jewish spirituality, nurtured by historical ideals and cultivated by moral discipline. Moses inspired it; the prophets tamed it; the sages uplifted it. It aims not for physical survival *per se,* but for the dynamic revival of the Jewish spirit.

And Ahad Ha'am spelled out the practical implications of his theory. The Zionist program must place emphasis on spiritual depth prior to organizational scope and political action, if the Jewish character and promise of Zionism are to be unfolded. Zionism is national in aim, ethical in essence, spiritual in content and universal in scope.

III

It is the enigma of Zionist history that the westerner, Herzl, living in comparative freedom and security, should be primarily concerned with the physical plight of Jews, while the easterner, Ahad Ha'am, residing in an environment of repression and violence, should direct his energies toward the alleviation of the spiritual plight of Judaism. Upon further analysis, it is evident that the one whose spiritual roots were deeper and whose environment more intensely Jewish would place the problem of assimilation before anti-Semitism. Herzl was an assimilated and alienated Jew whose Jewish consciousness was awakened by the shock of the Dreyfus affair with its blatant anti-Semitic overtones. Ahad Ha'am was a man spiritually and psychologically anchored in the living waters of historical Judaism. To Herzl, Zionism offered the solution to Jewish homelessness; Ahad Ha'am regarded it as an answer to cultural disintegration. The latter observed that with the advent of political emancipation Orthodoxy lost its hegemony, and protective Jewish isolation was reduced. The nation was losing its spiritual immunity and becoming subject to the lure and mirage of foreign culture. Dispersed throughout the globe without a centripetal force, groups of Jews will tend to be molded by local influences, with the resulting fragmentation into territorial units and ultimate disappearance as an ethnic entity in the process of social and cultural integration. Confronted with a new challenge which previously had not been faced by an insulated Jewry fortified by a way of life totally apart from its neighbors, Ahad Ha'am concluded that the Jewish people is in need of new cohesive forces and creative sources for survival. Its ever-present "will to live" seeks new forms. The threat of assimilation may suggest segregation as an escape, but, as expressed in Thomes Wolfe's phraseology, "You can't go home again", the Jews cannot return to the ghetto, physical or cultural. There is an alternative which avoids the evils of both extremes. In healthy inter-group relationships there is room for fruitful interaction. The reciprocal influences exerted evoke creative emulation in preserving and developing cultural values and institutions. What has been borrowed from an alien setting is recast in the image of the group to suit its purpose and express its spirit.

> We have gone through two successive periods, a long one of complete segregation and a short one of self-effacement . . . We are coming to recognize that salvation lies along neither of these two roads but along a third road that lies between them: that of the enrichment of our national individuality by means of imitation of the competitive kind.[105]

The Jewish people can develop an indigenous and modern Hebrew literature, and create its music and art together with institutional forms and social processes which will emulate the best of their environment.

Ahad Ha'am postulated a "will to live" as an essential component of his theoretical structure. Influenced by Darwinian biological concepts, he applied the "struggle for survival" of biological evolution to national history, suggesting the existence of a corporate national will, operating overtly and covertly through the chain of events. To nourish this "will to live," which (he claimed) had recently become dormant, is the function of the Zionist movement. The egotistical interest of the individual merging with the survival interest of the group—a value initially postulated in Mosaic Judaism, where reward is always corporate rather than individual—can be given new vitality in the context of modern Jewish nationalism.

Thus Palestine, rebuilt as a national home, will serve two significant ends indispensable for survival:

(1) A Hebrew environment without competing influences will enable a reconstituted Jewish majority to embark upon a spiritual revival as a link in the golden chain of the historical heritage.

(2) A spiritual center, Vatican-like in influence rather than authority, from which will emanate books and ideas in the Hebraic spirit and tongue, will create a bond between the outlying sectors of the vast periphery, materially assisting the center and spiritually benefiting from it. Authoritative without being authoritarian, the Land of Israel will once again assure the creative unity of the Jewish people. There was no equivocation in Ahad Ha'am's definition of the "spiritual center":

> A "center of our nationality" implies that there is a national circumference, which like every circumference, is much larger than the center . . . The majority . . . in the future

> (will be) scattered all over the world, but no longer broken up into a number of disconnected parts, because one part —the one in Palestine—will be a center for them all and make them all into a single complete circumference. When all the scattered limbs of the national body feel the beating of the national heart restored to life in its native home, they, too, will once again draw near to one another and welcome the inrush of living blood that flows from the heart.
>
> "Spiritual" means that this relation of center and circumference between Palestine and the lands of the disapora will of necessity be limited to the spiritual side of life. The influence of the center will strengthen the Jewish national consciousness in the disapora . . . it will give to our Judaism a national content which will be genuine and natural, unlike the substitutes with which we now try to fill the void.[106]

In accepting the continued existence of Jewish communities in their respective habitats throughout the world, Ahad Ha'am's formula for the unified and dynamic survival was designed to combine political realism with spiritual goals.

IV

The Zionist debate was three-cornered. Herzl championed political action directed toward the establishment of an independent state. A. D. Gordon called for economic reorientation and individual rehabilitation in the formation of a new rural society. Ahad Ha'am concentrated upon a new education that would pave the way to a spiritual revival. Though not exclusive of each other, one approach has frequently been emphasized at the expense of the others.

Cultural Zionism, as Ahad Ha'am's views became known, originally demanded a shifting of Zionist effort from mass recruitment under a political banner, to the less spectacular, slower process of education,—"the preparation of the hearts." He advocated an idealism anchored by the weight of intellectual comprehension and conviction rather than captured in the flight of fanciful slogans and grandiose plans. He demanded the total commitment of the few endowed with the persistency and perspective required for pioneer initiative in the new land. Critical of the various colonization projects dependent upon Baron Rothschild's philanthropy, he urged a concerted effort at organizing schools and cultural and educational enterprises directed toward a sounder Jewish awareness and national consciousness. Under his influence, the *Hovevei Zion* of Russia supported new schools in the Palestine colonies and, after 1902, added other educational projects to its agenda.

Ahad Ha'am's philosophy was all-encompassing, reaching beyond the domain of Zionist tactical strategy all the way to a definition of the function of literature. He was engaged in polemics with younger authors on the scope and function of modern Hebrew literature. When a spate of rising novelists, poets and essayists advocated broadening the horizon of Hebrew literature to include the artistic expression of values alien, and in some instances contradictory to historical Judaism, Ahad Ha'am opposed them. He insisted that the national revival must have its spiritual roots in the cumulatively selective heritage and experience of the Jewish people. The new literature, he maintained, must be Hebraic in content as well as in form.

The problem of Jew-Gentile relationship was not to be ignored by Ahad Ha'am's comprehensive analysis of the Jew in the modern world. The Jew's response to the non-Jewish environment impinges upon his self-image and his attitude toward his religion and his people. It affects his personality and influences his philosophy of life.

Ahad Ha'am was incisively critical of the German-centered Reform movement which sought to reconstruct radically the Jewish way of life. The remodeling, streamlined to the tastes of the times, necessitated the removal of all conventional furnishings, and called for their replacement by imitations of the Christian sanctuary and home. The Russian *Haskala* had concentrated upon a superficial dusting and polishing of the House of Israel to make it seem more attractive. German Reform, however, aimed at overhauling the entire structure. Both were moved by the desire to make the grade and be accepted in a gentile world. In contrast, Ahad Ha'am was primarily motivated by considerations of the authenticity and inherent value of Jewish sancta, without regard for outside approval. This, to him, was the path of dignity followed by free men; the other was the road of humiliation taken by the lesser breed:

> Terrible indeed is the backwardness, the degradation and the poverty that surrounds me here (in Russia); and well may I look for comfort across the border to the land in which there are Jewish professors and members of Academies, Jewish generals and statesmen. But when behind all the grandeur and the glory I discern a two-fold slavery, moral and intellectual, I ask myself whether I envy these Jews their civil rights; and in all truth and sincerity I answer "No, a thousand times no!" I will have none of them. I have no civil rights, but at least I have not sold my soul for civil rights. I can proclaim aloud my feeling of kinship with my fellow Jews, wherever they may be, without having to defend it by far-fetched and unsatisfactory excuses . . . I have no need to idealize my people and to pretend that it is superior to all others in order to justify its existence. . . . I can even adopt "the scientific heresy that bears the name of Darwin" without any danger to my Judaism. In a word, I belong to myself, and my opinions and feelings are my own. And this freedom of the spirit—scoff who will—I would not exchange or barter for all the civil rights in the world.[107]

An eloquent plea that has not lost its appeal with the passing of years!

V

Fishel Lachover, author of the definitive History of Modern Hebrew Literature, attributes to Ahad Ha'am the achievement of complete integration of ancient Judaism with twentieth century thought. "Without retreating from fundamental Jewish concepts, he redefines them in socio-national terms of universal context compatible with a modern intellectual perspective."[108] Whether religionists will agree completely with this evaluation is questionable. Nevertheless, contemporary Jewish religious philosophy is considerably influenced by Ahad Ha'am. In American Judaism, the Conservative movement regards him as a "source from which the movement has learned much."[109] Another Conservative spokesman is more generous in his credit: "And it was within the hospitable compass of the Conservative movement that the seeds of Ahad Ha'amism found their most fertile soil."[110] The important fact remains that for secular Jews he bridged the gap between tradition and modernism, between the Jew and the world. In the never-ending discussion on Judaism versus Universalism, Ahad Ha'am demonstrated that the universal reveals itself through national forms, and that Judaism represents the noblest in both, without inner contradiction. In their ultimate application, the universal elements in the Jewish heritage elevated it to a world religion.

A philosophy of such dimensions encompassed all of Jewish life, psychological and intellectual, individual and collective, in Palestine and abroad. It was directed toward a world-wide Jewish renaissance in the twentieth century, fostered and replenished by the spiritual center in Palestine—with whatever suitable political and economic conditions are required for its realization. The exponent of spiritual Zionism

> saw the national movement as the latest in the long evolution of the Hebrew spirit. . . . It can grow . . . where the Hebrew spirit can assert itself freely unhampered by foreign influences. Zionism is therefore synonymous with Judaism itself. Ultimately, Palestine would become not merely a state of Jews, but a Jewish state.[111]

It was Ahad Ha'am's cherished dream to compose his *magnum opus* on the ethics of Judaism. This was to be a comprehensive work presenting the philosophy of Judaism for modern man and also to serve as a contemporary summation parallel to ancient and medieval anthological restatements of the religious tradition. He never achieved it; but the bricks for this projected edifice are in the numerous essays which he produced over a period of thirty years. These are still useful materials for the rising structure of society and culture in Israel today.

VI

No discussion of Ahad Ha'am would be complete without some reference to the impact of his philosophy on Jewish education. This is especially so since the road to Zion, according to Ahad Ha'am, led through the vistas of the new education. His interpretation of Jewish historical experience and spiritual destiny contains definitive and far-reaching implications for education on all levels. Jewish schools in Europe, Palestine and—to a considerable degree—America, have been based on and guided by principles derived from the philosophy of spiritual Zionism. Four of Ahad Ha'am's major insights and corresponding applications are of particular relevance to Israel society and education and to Jewish communities abroad. His fundamental teachings, reformulated by his followers would suggest the following:

a) *The aim of Jewish education is to include the highest human and universal values embodied in Jewish ethics and conveyed by the literary and ideational content of the Hebrew spiritual tradition and Jewish historical experience.*

In fostering the values of the spirit and intellect, the Jewish school must assiduously avoid the pitfalls of chauvinism and narrow pragmatism marking the educational path of smaller and sometimes larger embattled nations. Ahad Ha'am's brand of Zionism, unlike that of some of his contemporaries, was not aimed at remaking the Jewish people in the mold of other nations, but to maintain and accentuate Jewish uniqueness and differentness.

b) *Authentic Jewish education instills a sense of belonging and meaningful identification to the extent that the individual attains fulfillment in the aspirations, ideals and achievements of the Jewish people without ignoring his own personal needs and the intellectual challenges of the times.*

These educational propositions flow directly from Ahad Ha'am's views on the ethical foundation of Judaism, its corporate character, and the Hebrew medium through which it has been expressed. They bridge the gap between the individual, the group and universal values, charging the educational process with the mission of Jewish survival and establishing the indispensibility of the Hebrew language as its vehicle of communication and inspiration.

c) *Jewish education in modern times, removed from the theology and methodology of the traditional curriculum, is yet to represent historical continuity in linking a redirected present and reconstructed future with the past.*

The apparently platitudinous character of this statement disappears in the light of vociferous pronouncements to the contrary by other spokesmen for the Zionist program both in Ahad Ha'am's day and in contemporary Israel. His was the profound conviction that emphasis upon eternal verities, national loyalty and historic continuity, does not run counter to the quest for scientific truth, individual freedom and human dignity. They are parts of the whole. Together they make for the wholesomeness of the new Jew-human being, prepared to stand his own ground in the face of the allurements as well as the rebuffs of the alien environment.

d) *In the open society, Jewish education is directed toward self-acceptance as against the sense of inferiority often infecting the less committed Jew in his role as a member of a minority everywhere except in Israel.*

To what extent are these imperatives reflected in Israel education today? The least that can be claimed for the first three (the fourth applying to education in the diaspora) is that they point up the normative if not the descriptive. The Hebrew University in Jerusalem has aspired to become that reservoir of spiritual values capable of feeding the tributaries in the world Jewish community as envisaged by Ahad Ha'am. It has successfully embarked upon expanding educational ventures benefiting Jewish students from abroad and, in increasing numbers, non-Jews from the emerging nations in Africa and Asia. The Weizmann Institute in Rehovoth, in its dedication to pure science and pioneering research, is another aspect and further extension of Ahad Ha'am's vision. Universal compulsory education, the gradual broadening of educational opportunities, the emphasis upon Bible and Hebrew literature, the sense of a historical link with the ancient past, the reinterpretation of hallowed texts in a contemporary intellectual frame of reference, the identification with the world Jewish community, the stubborn adherence to the democratic way of life and system of government in the midst of Near Eastern despotism (of both the right and the left)—these were all in the master's blueprints. The introduction into Israel public schools of the "Jewish Consciousness" curriculum with its enriched religious content elements drawn from Jewish tradition, would have received Ahad Ha'am's blessing.

Israel today is gradually becoming the spiritual center of a world-wide Jewish circumference. Hebrew teachers from Israel are sent abroad. American institutions of higher Jewish learning are setting up residence study programs in Israel. Numerous Israeli publications flow to all parts of the world. Pilgrimages, especially of young people from Europe and America, converge in Israel every summer. Ambitious Hebrew encyclopaedic projects are well under way (universal, juvenile, biographical, linguistic, Biblical and Talmudic encyclopaedias). Ancient and medieval classics are edited and published. These are among the numerous ventures in scholarly and literary creativity that have restored Israel's role as the centrifugal force in an international Jewish periphery.

But the promise is yet to be fulfilled. The military vigilance imposed upon the nascent state by the open hostility of its neighbors, compounded by the economic, social and cultural problems in the wake of unparalleled mass immigration is hardly the optimum condition under which the spirit can flourish. Nevertheless, the translation of Ahad Ha'am's ideas into realities, both in the character and image of Israel and in its impact on the world Jewish scene, is still the proclaimed goal of Zion and Zionism.

Leon Simon, a disciple, a member of the intimate circle

in the London period of Ahad Ha'am's life, and an expounder of his ideas, offered this tribute in his definitive biography of the master:

> Not only did he become one of the foremost Hebrew writers of his day, but . . . he saw the views for which he had fought gain wide acceptance. . . . By Zionists and non-Zionists alike he was widely recognized as a teacher whose breadth of view transcended the conflicting ideologies which threatened to disrupt the unity of the historic Jewish people, and in whose synthesis the claims of traditionalism and progress, of East and West, of religion and nationalism were reconciled.[112]

Yet, in the perspective gained over the forty years since his passing, Ahad Ha'am has been proved wrong on many scores. Unlike other Zionist leaders he could not anticipate the eventual indispensability of a physical haven of refuge for millions of Jewish survivors from the Nazi holocaust and Arab persecutions. One of his basic postulates, "the national will to live" operating within the world Jewish community as the prime factor in Jewish survival, appears to have little psychological or sociological basis.[113] He had little sympathy for the two paramount forces in the upbuilding of Israel—the emergence of a Jewish labor class and the *kibbutz* experiment in communal life. In addition, his idea of gradualism in attaining the Zionist goals was not justified by the cataclysmic events of the Second World War era.

This is no inconsequential list of misjudgments, particularly for one eager to accept for himself and his people the charge of the Prophets. Nevertheless, Ahad Ha'am emerges as one of the most important figures in Jewish history and among the major influences in modern times. Ironically, he apparently has made a greater contribution as a philosopher of Judaism than as an architect of Zionism.

For the contemorary Jew, Ahad Ha'am's views help to:
—define the character of Jewish religion;
—formulate Jewish values;
—heighten the appreciation of religious forms and institutions;
—illuminate the nature of Jewish historical experience;
—refute assimilationism by providing an ethical antidote to classical Reform universalism;
—offer a deeper insight into the nature of Biblical prophecy;
—spell out the Jewish intellectual confrontation with Christianity.

Ahad Ha'am continues to speak to Jews in terms of goals significant and relevant to a generation concerned with defining its relationship to its forebears, its encounter with contemporary issues and its responsibilities to its descendants. Thus

> . . . he made the profoundest impact on his generation. . . . prophet or not, he performed for his own generation a vital part of the prophet's function. It fell to him, on the threshold of the modern Jewish national rebirth, to reiterate the message of the ancient Hebrew prophets who warned their people against succumbing to the temptation to foreswear its consecration to universal ideals for the sake of immediate satisfactions. . . .[114]

REVOLT OF THE INDIVIDUAL

Micha Yoseph Berdichevsky

I

Zionism can hardly be defined as a rejection of the Jewish heritage. Neither can it be regarded as a negation of the Jewish ethical tradition, nor a substitution of western materialism for historic Hebraic idealism. Yet, this was essentially the message of Micha Yosef Berdichevsky—a moving spirit in Zionist thought and Hebrew literature.

Berdichevsky appeared on the Jewish scene in the role of a dissenter from the prevailing consensus. Before him, Herzl, founder of political Zionism, had begun to understand the importance of "a return to Judaism even prior to a return to a Jewish land." This was also stated with clarity and unequivocation by Ahad Ha'am, philosopher of Cultural Zionism who was not prepared to accept the Zionist formula without priority to a "spiritual center" dedicated to the furtherance of the teachings of Judaism. To Jewish historical values, in their traditional forms or modern reformulations, Berdichevsky responded with a resounding, dissenting negative, bringing a novel and revolutionary ingredient to the proposed Zionist solution. No wonder that Berdichevsky's novels and essays, rejecting passionately all that was accepted as valid and valuable to Jewish life and thought, have been for the most part confined within the domain of Hebrew letters! Yet no adequate appreciation of the character of modern Israel is possible without an understanding of Berdichevsky, the Hebrew novelist and essayist who pleaded so passionately for a new Jewishness without Judaism.

The voice of Micha Yosef Berdichevsky was responsible for the one note of discord in the chorus that heralded the new nationalism in modern Jewry. His was the cry for individualism in an age echoing with slogans of national purpose and collective solidarity. As a Zionist who rebelled against classical Judaism and normative Zionism, Berdichevsky was a major participant in the Zionist debate and became a chief contributor to the emerging Zionist synthesis. Paradoxically, this Polish-born, brilliant and sensitive soul who spent his creative years in Germany was inexorably opposed to the spiritual, cultural, religious and historical foundations for Jewish national revival. He challenged vigorously and vehemently the ideology advocated by Ahad Ha'am who was the leading exponent of historical continuity and spiritual emphasis in the Zionist formula. Decades later, when Berdichevsky was no longer on the scene and after the founding state of Israel, his nonconformist negations reappeared as outspoken assertions by small but most articulate elements in Israel society and literature.

II

Berdichevsky was born in 1865 in Miedzyboz, a small town in southern Poland, the birthplace of Israel Baal-Shem, founder of Hasidism. His father was a rabbi and the family traced its rabbinic lineage through many generations. Three family and environmental influences in his childhood proved potent factors in the molding of his personality and ultimately were reflected in his mature thought and writings. The first was the Hasidic spirit with its unleashed religious emotions, its profound inner experience and unbridled outer expression which often lifted him to the soaring peaks of poetic fervor or plunged him into the chasms of introspective probing and anguish. The second factor was a stepmother acquired when he was at the impressionable age of eleven; the unhappiness he suffered because of her lack of understanding and sympathy caused him to become overly sensitive and acutely responsive to individual needs and problems. The third element was his stifling, hemmed-in Ghetto upbringing in the crowded Jewish quarters set apart from the verdant homesites in the Gentile neighborhood which held a special attraction for the tender child, and fostered within him an insatiable hunger for nature and beauty. These became the foundations for the three pillars of Berdichevsky's philosophical and artistic structure: Emotion, Individualism and Aesthetics, in contrast to his illustrious adversary, Ahad Ha'am, who established his system on Reason, Nationhood and Ethics.

Reared in an atmosphere of study, Berdichevsky acquired extensive Jewish learning while secretly imbibing the new literature of the *Haskala* (Enlightenment). His marriage at the age of sixteen did not interrupt his pursuit of learning. He continued to study diligently, his lodging and maintenance provided for, as it was the custom, by his father-in-law. Shortly thereafter he was discovered reading a Hebrew secular book, and because of this he was driven out of the house. He chose to continue his education at the famous rabbinical school of Volozhin, and soon began publishing short stories and scholarly essays. At the age of twenty-five he went abroad to German and Swiss universities where he successfully prepared for a doctorate in philosophy. His dissertation dealt with the relationship of ethics to aesthetics, a point of departure which gave rise to fruitful thought in subsequent years. By this time he had already broken with his Orthodox upbringing, substituting for it—with great enthusiasm—the then popular philosophy of Nietzsche, which he grafted onto a secular nationalism to be applied to the Jewish scene. This goal he pursued in writing for the rest of his life.

Berdichevsky emerged on the Hebrew literary scene as a master of fiction and a challenging contributor to contemporary Jewish thought. His novels depicted the shocking, sordid and stultifying conditions of life in Eastern Europe where the individual was caught between the dictates of society and the passions within himself. Though essentially a Hebrew novelist, he was also a man of great erudition who produced several scholarly and philosophical works in German and was the author of short stories in Yiddish. In addition, he sought out the by-paths of Jewish lore, treasures of myth and legend deviating from the mainstream of normative Judaism, which he assembled and edited in Hebrew anthologies still definitive in our day. Essentially, however, he emerged as the spokesman for the young rebels who sought to broaden the intellectual and literary horizons of Hebrew literature. These formed a third force which, seeking to recast the religious heritage in a contemporary secular mold, rejected the existing forces of the "establishment": the commitments of the Orthodox camp on the one hand, and the reformulations of the modernist school of Ahad Ha'am on the other. A prolific author, Berdichevsky remained an original thinker and acclaimed novelist until his untimely passing in 1921 at the age of fifty-six.

III

In a recent book entitled *Modern Hebrew Literature—Trends and Values,* Professor Simon Halkin of the Hebrew University of Jerusalem, claims that "no understanding of the miracle of present-day Israel is possible without some understanding of the world of Berdichevsky."[115] He was the great rebel of Hebrew thought, the challenger without peer, whose doubts, heresies and restlessness, as conveyed in fiction and essay, have made him a commanding figure in a revolutionary age. His protest and dissent contributed toward the crystallization of fundamental affirmations in the Zionist synthesis. His life-long controversy with Ahad Ha'am and the latter's disciples, was unfolded in the leading periodicals of his day. Personally, Berdichevsky stood aloof from parties, platforms and programs. While engaging in heated polemics on the literary front, he always remained withdrawn as the secluded artist and thinker. Yet his voice was clear and audible in the Zionist debate.

The Zionist movement had rebelled against prevailing realities in the name of historic ideals. Protesting against the aberrations of Jewish life, which had been induced by the abnormal status of a permanent minority deprived of opportunity for secure and wholesome living, Zionist theoreticians appealed to the spiritual values in the cumulative experience of a people yet to fulfill its destiny in its ancient homeland. The Zionist idea represented continuity rather than severance of historical bonds. It sought to interpret and channel Jewish aspirations into historically determined, religiously dictated and pragmatically required avenues of operation. Though divorced in practice from the religious discipline of Orthodoxy and removed intellectually from its frame of reference, Ahad

Ha'am, intellectual leader of Zionism, accepted the spiritual demands of Jewish tradition and attempted to reveal, analyze and affirm their relevance. It was not so with Berdichevsky. With all its modernism, the prevailing mood of normative Zionism was a decided "yes" to Jewish values. Berdichevsky uttered an emphatic "no".

A further distinction: The architects of Zionism deplored the disintegrating structure of Jewish society. They criticized the inferiority status, resented the crippling passiveness to hostility and challenged the parrot-like acculturation to an alien environment. But they affirmed their allegiance to the inspired ideals of the ancient prophets and sages in Israel. Berdichevsky, in contrast, *questioned the very spiritual foundations of historical Judaism.* He did it, however, as an insider—"His Majesty's Loyal Opposition"—committed to preserve the corporate unity and entity of the House of Israel, thereby remaining the great dissenter instead of becoming the renegade that so many lesser talents proved to be.

Berdichevsky was obsessed by the burden of the past and desired to be relieved of it. He felt that dominance by the past dictated the people's mode of life in the present, stifling any creative initiative. It was not only the conventionalists who were chained to the past; the modernists, too, were bound to its spirit. To Berdichevsky, the history of the Jews in exile presented a depressing view of enslavement to yesterday and estrangement from today, all subject to a self-imposed predetermination of behavior and events by an age that had long since passed.

> We are an ancient people, submerged by too much inheritance, by a deluge of thoughts, feelings and values transmitted to us, so that we no longer can live our own lives, just be ourselves; our dreams and our thoughts are not our own, our will is not the one implanted in us; everything

> has been taught to us long ago, everything has been handed down to us. Everything is defined and confined within set limits and boundaries, measured and weighed, ruled and legislated; so that those among us who crave to find themselves are lost . . . they never can discover themselves.[116]

The individual is helpless in such a setting. His desires and yearnings, his very problems are suppressed and ignored. The heritage of the past has become more than the foundation for erecting the structure of the present. It is a prison wall preventing free movement toward the beckoning opportunities of the new age.

> For we are the slaves of our memories, the slaves of our inheritance. We have been mummified by thoughts transmitted and delimited . . . The past has shut out the present, taking from us the treasures of today while making us the porters for the burdens of yesterday.[117]

And Berdichevsky cries out, in anger and anguish: "We've had enough of it!"

He strikes out at "the book," from the Bible to all the vast literature of legalistic and pietistic commentaries and super-commentaries which command exclusive loyalty down through the centuries. The result has been an over-intellectualization and over-spiritualization at the expense of observing, enjoying and experiencing life at its fullest. Jews have been bogged down by the book which has blocked their view of life and removed them from reality. The emphasis has always been upon ideas rather than on people, and "Jews were replaced by Judaism."

> Our human form has been diminished to the extent that our political and national forms have been reduced . . . and we have become creatures who only stand and look into the book, see and turn only to their script . . . Noble feelings, great ideas, will and desire, all that beats within a

man's heart making him a man—a thinking, feeling and willing being—life in its fullness, everything has been suppressed by the sheer weight of the book.[118]

Berdichevsky sees no reason for continuing in that state of servility. "New needs and desires awaken within us." It is not necessary for us to be heirs; we can seek our own fortunes and hit upon new enterprises at will. We can refuse to remain the People of the Book and return to the Land of the Living. A total break with the past is both possible and desirable.

IV

It is disconcerting to read Berdichevsky, for like Shaw at his wittiest and most perverse, he enjoys standing everything on its head. Yet Berdichevsky is always serious and always startling. He is delighted with the things of which Jews have usually been ashamed; he is ashamed of what Jews have pointed to with pride.

Do the Jews boast of their compassion? Do they pride themselves on being peace-loving children of Abraham who was merciful? Berdichevsky is not impressed. He rejects entirely the existence of or the need for a separate Jewish morality that warrants our continued loyalty. He reminds us that physical courage and reliance upon the sword occupy a most respectable position in Biblical tales. An unbroken spiritual link from ancient Judea to contemporary Jewry is a myth that Berdichevsky wants to explode. "A concept of Jewish ethics is wishful thinking without foundation, as transient as all religious values."[119] He protests against the abstract spirituality which, in his opinion, Ahad Ha'am foists upon the Jewish people.

You have chosen a gracious and prepossessing Judaism, by dint of which we presumably exist and are allowed to exist;

> but we do not need the kind of existence whose merit is the cultivation of a sublime system of law and life. The Jewish people is a vital event, not the summation of some circumscribed abstract world.[120]

Such a revolutionary appraisal calls for a re-appraisal of Jewish history. To Berdichevsky, our ancestors were not heroes but cowards. The inspired acts of martyrdom in defense of religious convictions were futile gestures. Spiritual fortitude in face of danger was often a subterfuge for physical and psychological weakness. And the brave odyssey of centuries in exile was a tragic error of a crushed people, paralyzed into hopeless immobility, unable to take a last but noble stand to recover the lost ground, or else make a dramatic exit.

Berdichevsky takes up the cudgels against the Bible itself. The ideals of the Bible are of dubious validity. Monotheism, with its philosophic monistic ramifications, he regarded as a delimiting concept, inferior to the Greek pluralistic view of the world. Ethics in its prophetic uncompromising aspect was barren, consisting essentially of negations imposed to police human relations. Heathen aesthetics, on the other hand, was affirmative, containing an unfolding productive receptivity to life. Judaism as a religion was a historical error, and Jewish existence a catastrophe, reprehensible in its narrow horizon and restrictive denial of a real and full life.

The Jewish mission idea in both assimilationist and nationalistic versions—i.e., world-wide diffusion bringing the message of monotheism to mankind or advocating a return to the homeland to create a model society for others to emulate—is a deception. "In vain do we champion a noble ethical culture destined to be the light of nations, when it is dark in our tents and cloudy in our lives."[121]

In deploring domination by the past and enslavement to the book, with the lamentable effects of both of these, Berdichevsky keenly regretted the resulting subjugation of the individual in the interests of the collective. He reminds us that advances in the long history of Jewry were always scored by individuals whose accomplishments were largely not *because* of but *in spite* of the environment and the group. The *Gleichschaltung* in Judaism, the homogeneity of behavior, and the weight of tradition militated against individual differences and personal expression. He turned into a fault the very quality of historic Judaism accorded by Ahad Ha'am—its corporate nature and blending of individual interests and collective needs. He considered this frustrating and dwarfing to the image of man seeking to free himself from the manacles of custom and society. The spiritual tradition deadened man's sense of beauty and weakened his ties to nature. In becoming spiritual beings, Jews were transformed into emasculated men. Regarding this as the overpowering inheritance of catholic Israel, Berdichevsky

> battled for the right of the individual Jew who must free himself from the fetters of a narrow rabbinism and must regain freedom and self-assertion in all forms and phases of productive life.[122]

The fact that he borrowed much from Nietzsche did not in any way deter him; he had no preference for originality at the expense of quality. Merit and values do not recognize the boundaries of race and creed.

V

Had he stopped there, Berdichevsky would have been just another name in the rabble of rootless and confused intellectuals who constantly fall over their Jewishness without ever finding it. He came not only to destroy, but to build. And the edifice he raised was to be both functional and decorative for the household of Israel. Assimilation was the furthest thing from his mind, even if it went under the banner of integration. If Jews were to share equally in twentieth century life and thought, they were also to be separate. At this very juncture—the individual and his relation to his people—Berdichevsky made the transition from the negative to the positive:

> I saw that we build for ourselves too many castles in the air, that we are more spiritual than may be necessary, and that the spiritual consumes the physical in our people and makes us powerless. Then I developed the concept of a change of values. I thought of destroying the kingdom of the spirit and crowning the physical to restore to us vigor and courage so that we would be human beings on the pathways of life and not merely priests in the tabernacle. And then I saw that man is not alone; that a family cannot pave a road with no land at its disposal . . . that there is no people without a country. I rejected the condition of exile and dedicated myself to the unification of our people with its ancient homeland. . . .[123]

The starting point is a change of focus from religion to people, from group to individual, and from the spiritual to the temporal. Then enlightened self-interest of the individual becomes in turn the basis for intelligent group interest. Recognition by the individual of the factors that detract from his own security and freedom on foreign soil will compel him to seek personal fulfillment in the Land of Israel. Assimiliation offers no solution since it requires denial of self and the sacrifice of one's individuality in order to be accepted by an alien society. Zionism is the only answer to the personal quest, pointing to the opportunity for men to live freely and fully without having to be offered on the altar of the collective good. Only in a free Jewish society can the Jew be an unhampered individual. Thus Berdichevsky makes the *tour de force*: Zionism ejected on the basis of its idealistic historical foundations, returns in response to realistic individual needs. The outcome is not a rugged *laissez-faire* anarchism, but the harmonious blending of personal and social interests.

At first glance it would appear that Berdichevsky's subjective bias might be showing through as he dons the garb of objectivity and arrives at the Zionist solution via the route of supposed individualism.

The "change of focus" from the group to the individual is one of his major philosophical premises. "Man is the eye of the universe. The will of the individual is king over all propensities, the sum total of all potentialities."[124] This is a far cry from the Jewish spiritual tradition. Zionism predicated on this anthropocentrism becomes unequivocally a secular and secularizing movement. Berdichevsky has come to the parting of the ways in Jewish thought and has deviated from the main route. He declared:

> The aim is to establish anew the house of Israel on secular foundations . . . Zionism should stand up and say "No" to everything accepted heretofore. That which was found to support and reinforce survival in exile will prove a negative factor in the New Land. . . . The basic fallacy of Zionism was to link the new with the old. . . .[125]

The new man, Berdichevsky envisioned, motivated solely by personal considerations, will be compelled to seek a new life in Palestine. Freed from the inhibitions of a religious tradition, he can subscribe to any principle and entertain any theory without regard to its Jewish antecedents or contrasts. Unlike the Jew of the past, the Jew of tomorrow is at home in the real and natural world, appreciative of its physical phenomena, inwardly enriched by its contact. He is neither the "light unto the nations" nor is he their scapegoat. He is neither better nor worse than anyone else. Nor does he try to be better than others. He accepts all people for what they are and harbors no prejudice. Yet the Jew of tomorrow speaks the Hebrew language, for he must have a medium and it might as well be his own. He lives in Israel, for he would live in his own country. In all other respects, he is a citizen of the world.

> It is possible to begin again after fundamental changes in our lives and our hearts . . . There is no construction without prior destruction, and there is no being without ceasing.[126]

Thus, *the individualism of Berdichevsky led to nationalism that postulated both the Hebrew tongue and the land of Israel.*

His opposition to spiritual aspirations and cultural programs was, for all practical purposes, in consonance with the total dedication of Herzlian Zionism to the political goal of establishing the Jewish State. There was also formal agreement with Ahad Ha'am in the latter's insistence on a change of spirit as a prerequisite of Zionism. But to Berdichevsky, this meant a revolt against the spiritual rather than its re-affirmative development. Needed were radical changes, not mere palliatives. He longed for a return to the pre-historic force and vigor of the ancient Israelite tribes before they succumbed to the intellectual and the spiritual.

> I give you your thoughts and opinions, your doctrines and regulations . . . and you give me the body of ancient Israel, its natural and simple life. . . . Give us back our youth![127]

His was a romantic longing for pristine beauty, for primitive strength and simplicity—somewhat reminiscent of Rousseau.

Removing barriers, lifting controls, allowing life to take its natural course—these are values to be reflected in literature as well. In Berdichevsky's literary creed, the creative writer owes no obligation to the ethnic tradition. His spirit is not to be bridled by the harness of national culture. To Berdichevsky, Ahad Ha'am's attempt to create a literature imbued with the historic destiny and tradition of Israel, was anathema. His novels depict the conflicts of the individual, frustrated in his passions and drives, at war with the social mores. His essays champion the right of the individual to think and act with obligations to none. "We have room for all ideas and opinions. We may bow or refuse to bow to any deity of our choice."[128]

Yet, with all his untrammelled individualism, Berdichevsky—to borrow a term from Soviet vocabulary—was no "rootless cosmopolitan." So deep were his emotional ties that he found it extremely difficult to transgress the ritual restrictions of Jewish tradition. "When a Jew has given his life for the sake of a minor commandment, his blood cries out to me from the earth; when I transgress it, the image of this martyr rises before me."[129] There was an ambivalence within him: simultaneous detachment from and attachment to Judaism. His writings abound with personal confessions, often expressing deep anguish. He is fully aware of these paradoxes and recognizes them as the inevitable product of the peculiar condition of the Jewish people.

> A Jewish sadness raps upon the portals of my heart. I sit in my room and hear the restless moaning of the Jewish people, its protracted grief, hoary with age. . . . Within my

> being I feel the pain of my heritage, the aching of a life and a soul banished from paradise; I cannot break down that which I want to break down. . . . I crave unification, I want to create a new people—new human beings—and yet I am torn in my own soul. We are ripped to tatters forevermore.[130]

The sorrows of a nation are evident throughout his work—the sorrows of disturbing questions, aching problems and uncertain answers. He was the spokesman for a bewildered age.

Berdichevsky's untimely passing evoked the following tribute from M. Glickson, noted Hebrew editor:

> He fought for the new though his soul was caught between two worlds. An ancient heritage was alive and throbbing in his heart even at the time when he fought it bitterly . . . He was among the select few whom fate had charged to give form and expression to a generation in transition, in its being and becoming, its direction and destiny.[131]

VI

To what degree is Berdichevsky's influence felt in Israel today? Have his broodings and gropings withstood the test of time? Secularists, striving for a society released from religious dogma and institutionalized religion, invoke his name. Youthful rebels against social norms proclaim him their source of militancy. Some of the positive recognized ramifications of Berdichevsky's views are the emphasis upon individual needs and differences, the cultivation of the arts and physical development, the thrust for modernism in its negative as well as positive forms, *advant garde* literature, national pride and the striving for military preparedness. An important, but controversial concept is his negation of Jewish life and values of the two thousand years in exile. Segments of Israel society in its early stage of pre-State days adopted a critical attitude toward the diaspora, denying it the right and the possibility of survival. In recent years there have been attempts to discount Jewish spiritual merit beyond Biblical times, as expressed by no less a figure than former Prime Minister Ben Gurion in an address at Brandeis University.[132] The holocaust in Europe, revived in the memory of the present generation by the unfolding of the Eichmann trial, has tempered this reaction.

Of late a group of native Israelis has flirted with the cult of "Canaanism." It expresses itself in rejecting the values of Jewish historical experience and attempting to recapture some of the "naturalness" of ancient Hebrew and Canaanite paganism. Though it is not drawn directly from Berdichevsky, the disciples of this cult have found support and stimulation in his non-conformist doctrines.[133]

Again, on the positive side and paramount in the history of Zionism, is Berdichevsky's individualism which spelled out Zionism in personal terms. This was subsequently given deeper meaning by other creative minds and became a major element in the ideology of the pioneer youth movements—the *Chalutzim*—who dedicated themselves to the upbuilding of the land of Israel and the birth of a new society.

PSYCHOLOGICAL
READJUSTMENT

Joseph Chaim Brenner

I

A DECADE before the turn of the century there was only one organized political group among Jews, exerting an influence over not too large a following. A decade after the turn of the century there were more than half a dozen organized parties competing for the allegiance of an alert and conscious youth. In the short span of twenty years, hosts of young people infiltrated the ranks of Russian and Austrian liberal and revolutionary camps, creating their own platforms. It was a *Sturm und Drang* period characterized by emigration of masses, fermentation of ideas, and crystallization of forces. Nearly every important ideology still operative on the Jewish scene today received its initial formulation at that time. It was an age of slogans, programs, dramatic gestures and heroic deeds. Its atmosphere was charged with controversy, romance and the pioneering spirit. Statesmen, thinkers, poets and revolutionaries stirred the hearts of an attentive public whose constituents were sharply divided in their respective loyalties.

There was one man who saw the bleeding wounds of his

generation beneath its party emblems and heard the cry of pain above the din of words in the official slogans. A full participant in the rushing events of his day, he reflected the shiftlessness and restlessness of a Jewish *intelligentsia* caught in the whirlpool of social and psychological conflicts in a disintegrating Jewish society. He observed the individual hopelessly emerging from the swamp of yesterday only to be trapped in the quick-sand of today, doomed to failure in the feverish efforts to reach a solid footing. In response he descended to the bottom of disillusionment and despair and, paradoxical as it may appear, he planted the seeds of an imperative reaching upward toward hope and rehabilitation. In this way he offered a new, unattractive but compelling meaning to the Zionist definition. He was Joseph Chaim Brenner, novelist and publicist whose life, work, personality and death left an indelible imprint upon the mentality of a trail-blazing generation of pioneers.

Born in the Ukraine in 1881, Brenner early identified himself with the revolutionary movement, was drafted into the army, suffered imprisonment and managed to escape to London. His association with radical youth made him suspicious of platitudes and illusory dreams that offered no immediate relief to the vexing problems of economic insecurity and psychological maladjustment. His personal experience, combined with his heightened sensitivity fostered a critical, often skeptical attitude to social phenomena.

In London he edited, for a few years, *Ha-Meorer* ("The Awakener") which assumed unusual importance when the Hebrew publications in Russia were closed down in the wave of reaction that set in after the abortive revolution of 1905. At the age of twenty-eight, pained by ghetto life as he saw it in Russia and London, and discouraged by the meagre support for the literary venture he unselfishly fought to preserve, he made his way to Palestine hoping to find peace for his troubled soul.

> I will go to Palestine at the end of the year but only as a farm laborer. . . . I want to run away from all these holy and literary concerns. . . . I would like to do manual work and eat, drink, sleep and die in the field when my time comes. That is my one "ideal." I need some peace of mind if that is at all possible.[134]

Brenner's departure from Europe did not go unnoticed in Jewish quarters. Periodicals reported on "the famous Hebrew writer who suddenly rose and left the Diaspora to go up to Israel, and changed into a tiller of the soil."[135] But for Brenner, the promise of a new life remained unfulfilled for a long time. The talented writer proved a failure as a laborer. Reacting to the publicity abroad he wrote to a friend: "would you kindly note . . . that my happy days of work as a farm laborer numbered no more than six . . ."[136] He took up the pen again and held on to it until he met his death at the hands of Arab assassins in the riots of 1921.

During the twelve years of his sojourn in Palestine, Brenner came into contact with all strata of society and maintained a close relationship with labor elements. His extensive literary output included both fiction and essays on social and cultural issues. By dint of his personality and character he exerted a strong influence upon those who came into contact with him. He was a keen observer and incisive critic of all about him. The fact that he was the only literary figure of stature who had made Palestine his home was partly responsible for the centrality of his role among the pioneer elements. Seeing only darkness and degradation most of his life, with the passing of years he finally began to discern the light of a new and promising dawn.

II

Brenner's condemnation of Jews in the diaspora condition followed Berdichevsky's indictment of Judaism. To Western Reform, dispersion was a privilege, a *noblesse oblige* in the interests of monotheistic religion. To the traditionalist, it was a punishment for ancient sins committed in the Holy Land. To political Zionists, it was a calamity depriving generations of territorial and sovereign opportunities. To cultural Zionists, it was a fact to be reckoned with in the creative survival of the people. Brenner regarded it as a sin, not in the theological but in the human sense, a deplorable condition without moral justification. His short stories and novels graphically depict the degrading, fanatic, suppressing, unaesthetic and superficial in Jewish life. He decried the resulting poverty and depravity, the economic rootlessness imposed from the outside and the concomitant economic *luftmensch* form of existence. Such an atmosphere could breed neither healthy social values nor well-adjusted individuals.

Mere liberation from the confines of traditional authority does not automatically release powers constructive and remedial in themselves. The modern Jew may be intellectually removed from the ghetto, but that does not endow him with the social, economic and psychological environment essential to his well-being. The young Jewish intellectual presented a gloomy sight of conflicts and complexes, as he spouted cliches, became addicted to 'isms' and afflicted with basic maladjustments requiring radical treatment.

> I realized that his present life is no life. . . . I always understood his unfortunate role, impossible to bear. My first and last cry was for another foundation. . . . Then can we be saved from the disgraceful life we now lead.[137]

Brenner was not basically concerned with the political disability, social discrimination, cultural assimilation or religious repression of the Jew; these were impositions deeply felt and expressed by other Zionist spokesmen. He was primarily sensitive to the psychologically disintegrating and traumatic effects and the economic consequences on the individual personality. While Berdichevsky had stormed against the crushing burden of spiritual values which had been inhibiting individual freedom and development in the physical and aesthetic dimensions, Brenner conveyed the anguish and confusion of the Jew adrift in the muddy waters of the contemporary Jewish scene, polluted by the abnormalities accruing from minority status. To him, the pious slogans of diversified ideologies had little appeal. He dared to utter heretical doubts about the Zionist hypothesis in both its political and cultural phases.

> . . . I, the Zionist, am not talking about revival, spiritual revival, the Hebrew national spiritual revival, but only about exodus, the desire to escape from the ghetto. "Renaissance", "revival"—these are magic words but we have no room for them. . . . My Zionism asserts: the time has come for those of us most capable of living, to discontinue residing among others and blaming everything on the evil of others.[138]

He did not, therefore, resent Gentile hostility; it was a fact to be recognized. World Jewish dispersion in itself was the source, or at least the framework, of all evil; and nothing else was to be blamed.

Hence his quarrel with the socialists and cosmopolitans was not on nationalistic grounds, as in the case of his predecessors. Concerned as he was with grim reality, he never lost sight of the individual fumbling to find some anchorage in life. Grandiose ideas and eloquent generalizations failed to move him. There was an existentialist strain in Brenner's impatience with the glamorous phraseology and high-sounding verbosity of the political panaceas that flourished in sophisticated but restless circles. The class struggle of the socialists could not apply to a nation of petty storekeepers struggling to stay alive. International universalism ignored the problems of the little man beset with frustrations, befuddled with conflicts and taxed by pressures brought about by historical and contemporary factors. Behind all the pretentious terminology of these all-encompassing humanitarian programs he discerned among their zealous adherents a basic inferiority complex, a self-subjugation and overwhelming awe before the Gentile. They were frightened, self-deceiving Jews coveting approval and acceptance in an unfriendly environment.

Thus Brenner was not stirred by a great vision of anticipated glory, universal or nationalistic in scope, as were the statesman and visionaries of his day. His was a negative approach. He was running *away* from something when he left Europe, rather than running *toward* something when he arrived in Palestine. As one of the heroes in a novel of his, written in Palestine, calls out:

> I understand, in your case, the whole matter to be based on negation, a negative attitude to our life over there without seeing nor accepting anything positive here.[139]

Then follows the shocking accusation:

> You don't accept the entire Jewish people, do you?[140]

Herein lies the tragic enigma of Brenner's soul—an ambivalence toward his own people. The master, Berdichevsky, may have disliked Judaism, but he loved the Jew and fought to relieve him of the shackles of tradition in order to partake of the freedoms of modernism. The disciple, Brenner, who lacked the teacher's reverence for European civilization, chose to share lovingly the lot of his brethren, simultaneously resenting the deformed Jewish personality, revolting against organized Jewish life, and objecting to the sacred and the secular without distinction. His perspective took in only suffering, ugliness and deterioration everywhere. Jewry, having been on trial, had been found guilty.

In his scrupulous honesty, Brenner never mistook a gesture for the authentic act. Even the Zionist community in Palestine was a bitter disappointment.

> . . . If it were not so painful. . . this old community and especially the new, similar to the old. . . . These "negators of the Diaspora" of ours, who come here and make a new Diaspora. . . .[141]

In Palestine nothing had changed. Achad Ha'am had visualized the spirit of Zion overflowing to Jewish communties abroad. Brenner found the stifling air of the ghetto infecting the land of the fathers.

> The Palestinian reality frightened him into a cry of despair. "Why shall I then cling to the corners of the devastated altar!". . . The diagnosis was clear. "Our crisis is one of a people lacking the talent to live properly. Our farmers are pseudo-farmers. The Jewish intellectual who comes here eager to lead a different life, in its fullness, through physical work, scent of the field, soon discovers that he is not qualified for any physical labor. . . . Our crisis—that of our colonies and their workers, of the Jerusalem ghetto filled with invalids, paupers and fanatics—is only part of the general national crisis. Here is the destruction of a people in the simplest meaning of the term."[142]

Brenner's pessimism was far-reaching. There was a sense of the ominous in him. He stood alone among the personalities of his generation in the distrust of the twentieth century. Seeming to anticipate the cataclysmic events of the Nazi era that resulted in the annihilation of a third of world Jewry, he saw "darkened lands, great nations, many peoples, and among them a wandering sheep, a sacred flock heading for slaughter."[143] He felt a tense atmosphere and often spoke of the "last Jews." Writing a "long letter" he set out to prove that only disaster was in store for the weak stranger caught in the tentacles of blood-thirsty mobs.

Born in 1881, the notorious year marked by anti-Jewish riots, Brenner regarded himself as a child of the pogroms and was haunted by their spectre throughout his life. The sense of catastrophe accompanied him. Yet there is a clinging to life for all its worth, a strong urge for a little sunshine and cheer. The defeated, but uncrushed hero of his last novel prays to God: "Father of orphans, be good to me. Send me the rays of the sun, and I, the orphan of orphans, will accept your gift in gratitude, love and hope. . . ."[144]

III

What is the solution to these tragically perplexing problems? On the surface they appeared to add up to a hopeless situation. Yet, on the crumbled foundations of despair, a positive philosophy was established.

> His very denial of God, religion, and history, his social and personal conflicts, he had to make into inspirational sources for continuity and survival. . . . Brenner's atheism sets out to cancel all accounts, cancelling at the same time disap-

> pointments, faults, aberrations and falsifications in the individual and in society . . . in the long run, cancelling itself out.[145]

Zionism may not be *the* solution, but it has to be carried out. There is no alternative. Everything else has been tried and has failed. "Zionism is the belief in the possibility of the impossible," he maintained. The Jewish people has reached the end of the rope. Palestine is the last station in the trek of ages, the point of no return.

Brenner did not invent this mood; he reflected it. Much of this attitude, that of pessimistic positivism, contrived to make Israel what it is today. In the War of Liberation following the establishment of the State in 1948, the Israelis were said to have been in possession of a secret weapon. This they called *ein braira* ("no alternative"), which made victory the only remaining choice in place of total destruction.

The analogous rationale of existentialist thought again warrants mention at this point. The anguish of man, his helpless existence in a strange world, befriended neither by nature nor by any transcendental force in the cosmos, places a great burden of responsibility and maturity on his shoulders. Man, in his loneliness can rely on no one but himself. Thus, a negative philosophy becomes the basis for a constructive call to responsibility.

It would be wrong to claim that Brenner's argument was based solely upon a stubborn clinging to the impossible. He also pointed the way. The road to salvation was to be found in the realm of physical labor. He himself had attempted to become a laborer; the fact that he failed did not deter him from re-emphasizing its innate significance. In this he was influenced by A. D. Gordon, prophet of the "religion of labor."

Labor is not to be regarded only as an expedient form of activity necessary for the reclaiming of the land. It is endowed with a therapeutic power indispensable to the ailing Jewish personality. Physical work is productive. It offers continuity, purifying and pacifying. It represents an authentic expression of economic man, making for rootedness and stability, a kind of occupational therapy for the neurotic Jewish personality.

Interaction in the processes of production presents a creative experience, emotionally satisfying in the operational as well as the culminating stages. This is especially true of farm labor.

On assuming the editorship of a labor monthly entitled *Ha Adama* ("The Earth"), he states:

> "Ha Adama" means not only land and country [agriculture and statehood] but something else. The earth is our aim for rootedness in all areas of life . . . recognizing the foundations of reality . . . the pull to the source of renewal, the source of human truth.[146]

Thus, Brenner the novelist, offered a depth psychology alien to the context of an emerging nationalism. Brenner, the analyst, reveals an anti-Jewish bias unexpected in a resurgent nationalism. He focuses attention upon the individual, a strange emphasis in political nationalism. *These elements make the Zionist formula so intriguing and unique, substantially different from other nationalistic programs acted out in the world arena.*

Labor serves another worthwhile purpose in Brenner's scheme of things. It is an antidote for the ills of anti-Semitism. Exilic life, after the expulsion from the homeland some two thousand years ago, has become essentially unproductive. The "de-proletarianization" of Jewish masses, he claimed, caused anti-Semitism:

> An eternal hatred was implanted in the hearts of nations against those who came and used the fruits of their labor . . . yet separated themselves from them.
>
> The question of Judaism is the question of the absence of productive labor for the masses of Jews who have become like flying dust, unable to work.[147]

The revulsion against centuries of Jewish history coincided with the Zionist rebellion against life in exile. It made the rejection of the Diaspora complete, negating it in all existing manifestations. Palestine restored becomes a categorical imperative without which the history of the Jews comes to an ignoble end.

IV

In the light of these negative affirmations, Brenner's role in Zionism is more clearly defined. Already in the London interlude, he symbolically named his periodical, *Hameorer,* ("The Awakener"), designed to awaken the individual from the accommodating acceptance of the *status quo* and the uncritical espousal of popular causes. While some were battling traditional isolationist forms, and others were berating assimilationist trends, Brenner was challenging the current Zionist claims and demanding a deeper, penetrating definition of Zionism with a brutal frankness in its excruciating logic. The insights, doubts, conflicts, and glimmers of hope crystallized into a three phase position which can be regarded as a summary of Brenner's complex gropings:

1. *Honest self-assessment to the point of complete negation of any positive characteristics attributable to Jewish life.*
2. *A "nevertheless" attitude regarding the Land of Israel*

as the last station, and Zionism as an experiment in total revolution among the "last" Jews, to make them the first in the building of a new nation.

3. *Individualistic Zionism pointing to personal alignment with the Zionist program—in changing radically one's mode of life to comply fully with the two demands of immigration and proletarianization.*

His attitude to Jews and Judaism merits further elaboration: Pride in the values and institutions of Judaism was unjustified as far as Brenner was concerned. Historically, survival under adverse conditions was not brought about by spiritual courage; it was a by-product of weakness, cowardice, and a talent for adaptability. Martyrdom never achieved the purpose of inciting rebellion against the exilic form of existence and was of dubious holiness. There was therefore little inspiration in either Judaism or the Jews. The past, acclaimed as a heroic and spiritual odyssey, was to him "a bitter error, exaggerated pride and deception."[148]

Had Brenner stopped at this point he would have been no more than a case-study for psychiatrists, as was another Jewish genius, the philosopher-psychologist, Weininger, whose hatred of Jewishness compelled him to commit suicide. Brenner's negations, however, led to affirmations, with the hate sublimated into love. He said:

> With a thousand threads am I tied to my people Israel. . . . My life is linked with a strong bond to its life. . . . I love the Jewish masses and would therefore like to dedicate to them my whole life, work, energy and talents. . . .[149]

He was encouraged by the few examples of a new type of Jew rising in the Land of Israel, whose rejection of existence in exile was combined with a restoration of personality through the redeeming process of labor on the soil of the homeland. Such personal realization of Zionism was to make it a living and working faith.

Brenner not only preached but practiced. Unlike other men of his age, he did not live apart from but with his people. He influenced as much by his personality as by his writings. The author was one with his artistic creation.

> More than the grief, pain and calamity of the heroes of the stories, was felt the grief, pain and misfortune of the author himself. One sensed a full identification of the creator with his created. One felt a great truth, the person of the author as a man of stature and distinguishing features; a personality calling out, demanding, devoid of personal peace and disturbing the peace of others, an ethical personality. . . .[150]

He was a man of uncompromising honesty, a prophetic spirit committed to indivisible truth, motivated by a fanatic devotion to its dissemination. A follower of the doctrines of Tolstoy, he pursued the life of an ascetic, subscribing to vegetarianism, denying himself luxuries, and serving as a true friend to all who came into contact with him. The scope of his immediate influence was consequently considerable, especially among the workers. A labor leader of Palestine referred to him two years after his death as.

> our master and teacher, about whom it could be said, "surely our distress he did bear," who suffered our pains and had the power to open our wounds mercilessly, and through whom we were educated.[151]

His outward calmness and discipline notwithstanding, he was torn asunder within, always beset by doubts, never attaining harmony. He was too loyal a son of his people not to be shaken by its plight. The individual and the national reckoning blended in him to the point where the line of demarcation disappeared. This, in essence, was also germane to his philosophy.

V

It is obvious that Brenner's intellectual brooding and emotional outbursts, disguised though uninhibited in fiction form, are prone to be misconstrued. Anti-Semites may find authoritative support for defamatory charges. This accounts for the fact that Brenner is probably the only major Hebrew or Yiddish author of fiction whose work remained untranslated even in part.

In summary, Brenner contributed toward:

- a critical attitude to life in the Diaspora, the shortcomings of which are to be traced largely to psychological consequences of economic factors;
- a searching and groping for new content;
- an introspection, intellectual and emotional, ultimately a basis for renewal and reconversion;
- a nationalism without suppression of the individual, and an individualism coordinate with nationalism;
- an affirmation of labor (which was more fully developed by A. D. Gordon);
- a realistic pessimism serving as the foundation for a "no alternative" reconstructionism.

These insights and values were crystallized in his stream-of-consciousness fiction, essays and polemics during a life of exemplary dedication.

Nearly half a century after his tragic end, the name of Joseph Chaim Brenner is still revered, and his influence felt among the labor and *Chalutz* segments of Israel society today.

REDEMPTION OF THE SELF

A. D. Gordon

I

Zionism as a political movement was founded by Herzl. Its cultural renaissance was spelled out by Ahad Ha'am. The Hebrew language was revived by Ben Yehuda. The man who, more than any other individual, is identified with the social and spiritual foundations of modern Israel, is A. D. Gordon:

> . . . the Prophet of the Second and Third Aliyot . . . his words have been eagerly read, discussed, interpreted and misinterpreted, and have served Jewish youth as criteria for their deeds and thoughts.[152]

Aaron David Gordon merited the foregoing tribute by virtue of his preachment and practice during the formative years of Israel society in the first two decades of the nineteenth century. A combination of fructifying ideas, forceful personality and selfless behavior converged in one individual and set him up as the moving figure in a pioneering generation. The principles expounded by Gordon have become indigenous to the Israel socio-economic and educational environment. His contribution is most readily appreciated when the Jewish community in Israel today is compared with Jewish communities throughout the world.

Jewish life in the State of Israel differs radically from its counterpart elsewhere. With an autonomous society constituting its majority population, the Israel community is easily distinguishable from Jewish minorities in the Eastern and Western Hemispheres. The accoutrements of national and territorial independence in the form of government, language, social structure and legislation, present a flourishing civilization with little or no foreign infringement upon authentic self-directed growth. This, of course, is to be expected. Less obvious, but of equal if not greater significance, is the difference in values not specifically ethnic nor religious in origin. They relate to nature, labor, agriculture, the social climate and school curriculum. At least among the pioneer elements who represent the "true" Israel, interests and attitudes toward economic pursuits and personal happiness are at variance with those of co-religionists in other countries. The antecedent and prevailing spirit of modern Israel points to rural rather than urban living as the norm. Manual labor is often by choice rather than by necessity. In the hierarchy of gainful occupations, industrial arts take precedence over white collar professions. The farmer is held in high esteem and, as a rule, may partake of a cultural diet richer than that of the city dweller. Apparently, geographic transplantation has been accompanied by social transformation as the new twentieth century Jew emerges on his native soil. In this metamorphosis Aaron David Gordon played a leading role, through his philosophy, personality and example.

II

Born in Poland in 1857, Gordon led an undramatic life of comparative economic ease, without the material and psychological stresses and strains characteristic of the rise of other luminaries on the Jewish horizon of his day. In the years when he was employed as a land clerk, he devoted his spare time to study and the furtherance of the Zionist cause in his own community. Then, at the age of forty-eight, Gordon experienced a spiritual crisis which effected a turning point in his life. His age, family and position notwithstanding, he was moved by the power of his convictions to depart for the beckoning but desolate shores of Palestine. He spent the last eighteen years of his life as a farm laborer in various settlements in the Holy Land. It was during this period that Gordon became the mentor and symbol of the generation which brought about the great Zionist revolution, redirecting the course of Jewish history. He died in Palestine in 1922 at the age of sixty-five.

Herzl had diagnosed the Jewish problem in political terms of national statelessness; Ahad Ha'am defined it as cultural assimilation and group disintegration in the wake of emancipation; Gordon discerned it in the personal and psychological conditions of economic rootlessness and total urbanization of the individual. Once he had identified the malady, he decided to begin the remedy by applying the prescription.

Upon arriving in Palestine, Gordon turned down opportunities to teach. He was determined to serve as a night guard and farm laborer. Without adequate training or sufficient preparation, he made the difficult transition from the desk to the plough as he set out to live by his own faith.

What Gordon saw disturbed him—Arab labor tilling Jewish farmland, Arab guards protecting Jewish property.

To him, removal from direct contact with the soil through its cultivation disqualifies the proprietors of record from becoming owners in fact. Certainly, on the national scale, the land is owned by those who till and guard it themselves without benefit of proxies. This applies to industry as well. The country belongs to those who build it by the sweat of their brow.

> If we do not till the soil with our own hands, the soil will not be ours—not only not ours in a social, or a national, but even in a political sense. The land will not be ours and we shall not be the people of the land. Here, then, we shall also be aliens just as in the lands of the diaspora where, too, there are Jews who rent land, who buy fields, gardens and orchards, and traffic in the fruits of the labor of others. It is only to the degree that we here possess settlements and farms in which the work is done wholly by us that we shall become citizens and natives of the land.[153]

The reasoning is in line with the Marxist concept of ownership. It is nonetheless applicable in the reclaiming of a lost homeland. The very absence of Jews from heavy industry and agriculture, historical factors notwithstanding, placed the Jew in Europe in the vulnerable category of "foreigner," though in some instances as in Hungary, Jewish settlement predated its native population. Gordon insisted that residence in Palestine without changed economic conditions would not remove the stigma. In order to possess the land there had to be "conquest of labor." This called for willing employers and available employees—phenomena not too common in Palestine during the early years of the twentieth century. The arrival of hundreds of young idealists, intellectuals by training but workers by commitment, tipped the scales in favor of Jewish labor. The actual rise of an agricultural labor class was a long drawn-out battle against competitive cheap Arab labor, employers' distrust and physical unfitness and lack of vocational training on the part of Jewish laborers. Among the participants in that struggle are men who have led the State of Israel. They include Premiers Ben Gurion and Levi Eshkol and President Ben Zvi.

Gordon was not the only spokesman for this movement, though he was its philosopher. What distinguished him from the others was his seniority in years and his dedication to this strenuous life in spite of the limitations of a frail and aging physique. A prominent contemporary, in reminiscing about A. D. Gordon, stresses his singular devotion to physical work:

> When his efforts to work at digging ditches in a grove proved beyond his strength—he managed to dig three a day while some of the others did fifty—the young farmers of the colony offered him the position of assistant to the colony clerk, but he refused.[154]

The challenge of the moment can evoke great sacrifice for a worthy end. To sustain the sacrificial effort over a lifetime, however, the means in themselves must be worthy. Youth, when faced with the challenge of an attractive cause, will volunteer for physical labor over a limited period of time. An aroused patriotic sentiment can lead to inspired heroic acts—even to the extent of jeopardy to one's own life. But dedicating one's entire future to seemingly unprofitable and tedious toil involves more than courageous behavior in the face of danger. Physical work itself has to assume a new meaning and become spiritually rewarding and continuously replenishing. Such was the achievement of Gordon.

> It seems clear that a half-hearted urge to work just because there is nothing to lose, to work merely for the purpose of carrying on a national existence without the powerful

> inner conviction of the importance of this life, is so unstable, so narrow an aim as to be ineffective in transforming a youth who would like to be healthy but finds it very difficult to acquire health. We must, in spite of ourselves, seek another road.[155]

This road was paved by Gordon and his disciples when they elevated and transformed labor from required routine to the inspired privilege of a religion—the "religion of labor."

III

> A.D. Gordon laid the philosophic foundaion for the change in the Jewish estimate of the worth of labor . . . For Gordon . . . labor is not a curse upon one cast out from the paradise of idleness, an inescapable evil of civilization, but rather an ideal, a blessing upon him who has found favor in the eyes of the Lord.[156]

There were two standard views of physical work; Gordon introduced a third. In a normal situation work is accepted as matter-of-fact, a necessary component of economic reality. In the Jewish group, the transient state of its existence compelled it to rely on portable and consequently mental resources for a livelihood. Hence even skilled labor dependent upon raw material or instruments of production in any one locality was hardly an asset. In the course of history, manual labor was relegated to the category of necessary evil and regarded, in a sense, as detracting from the dignity of the individual. Gordon evolved a thesis on the spiritual powers of physical labor. He equated work with worship, as suggested by the Hebrew term *Avoda,* shared by both functions. Labor is endowed with an inherent nobility that elevates man above the animal. Physical energy expended productively and creatively strikes a responsive chord in man's soul. It is a process which releases forces within that are ennobling, fulfilling and revitalizing.

> You will derive pleasure from every task that you undertake, from every deed that you do—a pleasure like that which you derive in eating and drinking. . . .
> You will then know and consider in your heart that there is in work such spiritual wealth of which you can see only the barest fringe. . . .[157]

The Jewish people stands in need of this spiritual commodity produced by physical work. The circumstances of exile have imposed impoverishment of soul and diminution of person. Returning to the homeland is of little consequence unless it involves release from conditions similar to those imposed by the former environment and the adoption of a new and different way of life. And it is incumbent upon the Jew to change not only his locale but, by his own efforts, the very conditions under which he lives. Crucial to this new life are new forms of a livelihood.

> When you will utterly abandon the life that was created by others, give it up as completely as you have given up their land, and you will come to create here a *new life,* a life of your own, then the glowing ember will again be rekindled. . . .[158]

Productive labor is this new imperative. The regenerative force of work is two-fold: it will give nationhood back to the Jewish people and restore the individual to his full human stature. The benefits experienced in the process flow from the therapeutic potency of constructive labor as well as from its indispensability for the rebuilding of a homeland. "The reward of labor is inherent in the work; otherwise it falls short of its inate nobility."[159] It is therefore incumbent upon the individual to change his "mode of life. . . . to make it conform to the ideals of labor."[160] And Gordon did it, setting the example for others.

On the surface, a similarity with the Marxist dialectic of labor may be detected. The difference, however, is impressive. To Marx, economic value is created by labor. That is all that counts. Gordon was concerned with its spiritual ramifications. He ascribed to it a mystic power bringing man closer to the cosmic, attuning him to the divine and enriching his life with another dimension. The Jewish people is in urgent and dire need of it

> not only as a force to tie man to the earth and possess it, but also as a factor essential in the creation of a national culture.[161]

> Not an academic culture do we come to create today . . . but the culture of life . . . the beliefs and opinions of life, the art in life, poetry in life, ethics in life, religion in life . . . the living link between the present and the past . . . Our goal is to make with our own hands those things that make life.[162]

Thus shall Israel prove different from the dispersed Jewish communities in the world—creatively productive, spiritually and authentically unique.

> We strive to create in the land of Israel a new Jewish nation, not a colony of the nation in the diaspora, not a continuation of the diaspora in a new guise.[163]

The individual will find salvation and the people redemption in a mutually beneficial engagement where the one is not offered on the altar of the many.

IV

Labor is one side of the coin in Gordon's ideological currency. Nature is the other. A return to Israel, Gordon insisted, is to be a return to nature.

> And when, O Man, you will return to Nature, you will open your eyes on that day and you will gaze straight into the eyes of Nature, you will see therein your own image, and you will know that you have returned to yourself, that when you have hidden from nature, you have hidden from yourself.[164]

Then the Jew will again be himself, for to rusticate is not to escape; it is to come home again.

Gordon's nature-labor thesis is as follows: Contact with nature uplifts the spirit and enriches experience. Man is more human when he senses the beauty of nature in all its majesty and partakes of outdoor life in all its simplicity and freedom, unhampered by restrictions of city civilization. Deriving a livelihood from the cultivation of the bounties of nature is salutary to the spirit, purifying to the emotions, releasing to the mind and ennobling to the character. The broadened vision, the refined and overflowing feeling and the stimulated thought add to the capacity for getting the most out of life. Without it we merely survive; with it we are continually revived. "For we of today are far, and are continually moving farther away from the source of life, from Nature."[165] Reversing the process enables us to lead the good life. Then do we transcend ourselves and attain the harmony and unity of a higher form of existence. "Pure, natural life . . . amid Nature and with Nature. . . . expressing the sense of higher unity and higher responsibility—this is true religion."[166]

The landscape of Israel, with its historical associations and illusions, is all the more charged with appeal for wholesome human response.

> It seems as though here the fullness of divine abundance, emanating from all the cosmos into the soul of man and especially into the soul of the Jew . . . is altogether different than in the lands of the Diaspora. In the language of the soul . . . I would say that the essence of the infinite, the essence of truth, holiness, beauty, courage, the essence of all divine emanation is conceived by the soul in a different manner. . . . Here each one of the multitude of feelings, inclinations, desires and powers of the soul receives an illumination . . . different from other lands.[167]

Thus nature beckons to us to approach it, unveiling itself for those who choose to embrace it.

How is the gap between the Jew and nature to be bridged? Not by intellectual comprehension of the phenomena of nature, nor by the aesthetic perception of its grandeur, but by man's establishment of his domicile in its midst. This was Gordon's intention.

> The categorical imperative of the spirit of man, therefore, does not live in the glib phrase of the culture of today: "Know nature and love it." Rather is it to be found in the wordless notes, inaudible in our culture, of the voice that coos like a dove in the searching soul, that beats like the wings of a bird in its narrow cage: "Live Nature."[168]

Gordon asserted that the city retards human progress. The ills of mankind, social conflicts and moral deterioration are caused by withdrawal from the munificent blessings of nature and labor. To embark upon a life of labor in communion with nature is to combat the "conventional lies of civilization"[169] and ameliorate the complexes and complexities of modern times. Man's quest for freedom, his desire for untrammelled and creative expression, his search for wholesomeness and harmony, are found on the threshold of nature. In confrontation with nature, his potentialities are realized and his consciousness refined. He acquires a sense of belonging by becoming a citizen of the universe in addition to being a member of the human race and a son of his people. "The sum of all this lies here: to educate, to regenerate the Jew, one must begin at the beginning—with man."[170]

Gordon was undoubtedly influenced by Rousseau and Tolstoy, for he was a great admirer of the latter. Yet what he adopted, he adapted with the stamp of his own originality. To Rousseau, return to nature meant decontrol, loosening the bonds of behavior as imposed by civilization. To Gordon, it was a higher discipline spelling out greater and not lesser responsibility and spirituality. Tolstoy's anti-technological "return to the primitive"[171] was a far cry from Gordon's attempt to formulate a "religion of labor drawing from primary religious sources, from the source of a natural religious perspective, cosmic and ethical."[172] Much closer is the transcendentalism of Thoreau, but Gordon was not acquainted with the New England school of thought.

V

How is the new society, as Gordon envisaged it, to be achieved? Not in the conventional manner: "Our national regeneration is not restricted to the establishment of a new social order or given to a renewed social spirit."[173] The individual begins with himself. He is to change his mode of life to conform with these ideas. To live in Israel and speak Hebrew is a form of Zionism acceptable to the official spokesman for the movement, but inadequate as far as Gordon was concerned. To mold one's own life in consonance with the ideals of labor is the *sine qua non* for fulfillment of the individual and the rejuvenation of the Jewish people. There are no half measures. "For such an achievement in general, and for our nation in particular, one rule must govern: either there is a complete achievement, or none at all."[174] Obviously, the university student turned farmhand can hardly experience the joys of creative labor if he remains a wage earner in the employment of others. "Such an attitude cannot be expected from the so-called proletarian who is deprived of the right to enjoy the actual fruit of his toil and to stand in direct personal relationship to what he creates."[175] Only independent farming makes this possible.

In the Land of Israel this took a new untravelled course of greater promise. Economic necessity, an inhospitable climate and topography, security considerations and common ideology, all brought into being the unique agricultural collective which became indigenous to Israel and attracted world-wide attention. Though not directly its prime mover, Gordon influenced the Israel *kibbutz* as it blossomed forth in the post-war decades. It proved to be a chief factor in the upbuilding of Palestine and a most successful social experiment based upon Gordon's ideas on man, nature and labor. "Thus the ideas of labor and the collective became inseparably fused."[176] Gordon joined the first collective, Degania on the Jordan, when it was formed in 1909. And a world-wide youth movement educating toward collectivist living in Israel bore his name.

The "religion of labor" with its metaphysical overtones combines personal needs with national interests in the initial critical stage of nation-building. The individual's quest for meaning, expression and fulfillment by means of the dual process of physical labor and communion with nature is bound up with the emerging image of a Jewish people reborn. Gordon objects to Berdichevsky's imitation or even Ahad Ha'am's emulation of alien values and institutions. Genuine self-directed creative expression, not subject to dictation by outside factors, is his goal.

> We are in search of ourselves and our own way of life. Neither a sponge to absorb everything with nothing of its own except its sponginess, nor life translated from others or patterned after the cliches or in the spirit of others, but rather an independent personality—national for the group and individual for the person—living by its own spirit and creating a life of its own. . . .[177]

He therefore opposed socialist doctrine, especially in its class conflict format, considering it an alien growth. But he accepted, nevertheless, the socialistic concepts of "labor, national ownership of the soil and the means of production."[178]

His opposition to Marxism stems from his concern for the individual. A theory of history placing human events in the vise of determinism is unpalatable to one who puts the unfettered human spirit above dogma. "Man is not sacrificed, even on the altar of the Nation,"[179] Gordon asserted. Nor on the altar of Class! The individual is not a spoke in the wheel of historical necessity. His fulfillment, physical, social, intellectual, artistic and spiritual is primary. Man is an end in himself. In this Gordon leans heavily on the Jewish religious heritage.

> We are the goal *per se* . . . the goal or chain of goals begins with us and in our own lives from the day that we come to the land of Israel and commence to work.[180]

This framework of land and labor is the ideal setting for the blossoming forth of man's potentialities. But the Jewish pioneer-farmer is not the counterpart of the European peasant. The stereotype peasant, provincial in outlook, unsophisticated intellectually, limited culturally, was as remote from Gordon's goal as the urban merchant.

> In Exile, our life is not real living . . . since there is no room for achieving the goals essential to us in themselves . . . a life which is spiritual and material, national, universal and individual simultaneously.[181]

VI

We have been describing, without singling it out, the third pillar of Gordon's philosophical structure *self-fulfillment,* which he achieved and exemplified in the Palestine years, the final period of his life. "Personal realization" became the rallying slogan of a pioneer movement whose members converged on the homeland from all continents, the Americas included.

The dream of national restoration was born when the state was destroyed in 70 C.E. The Zionist movement in the nineteenth century was the political formulation of a religious aspiration, kept alive through the ages. It kindled the imagination of a people unwilling or unable to bear any longer the blows of persecution or the demands of emancipation. A generation liberated from the intellectual shackles of the ghetto found in the emerging Jewish nationalism a substitute for the religion of its ancestors. Like their fathers before them, modern Jews sought and hoped for personal salvation. In response to this quest, Gordon reinterpreted Zionism in personal terms, transforming a platform into a faith, and a goal into a promise.

Zionist action was no longer altruistic self-negation in the service of a noble and distant aim. Zionism was rewarding self-fulfillment, a realization of the spiritual powers of the individual in a new life, hectic but heroic, difficult but romantic, self-denying but fulfilling. A challenge had become an opportunity. The Jew was to be saved as the man in him drew from his own untapped resources, enabling him to regain his lost stature. A nation's destiny became an individual's career. The lines of demarcation between nationalism, humanity and individuality were blurred, and the three separate entities blended into one force. The national mission, the social gospel, and the personal interests, are parallel lines drawn in the same direction, converging at the horizon. This was Gordon's crowning achievement, and youth throughout the Jewish world followed his lead. Many could truly repeat after him: "The land of Israel has given me much life, as much as I can hold, to my fullest capacity in the enjoyment of life."[182]

To be conscious of light entails being aware of the darkness. There can be no acceptance of a new faith without rejection of a previous one. Gordon pointed to the grave deficiencies requiring corrective measures:

> The simple truth is forgotten or dimmed, that the basis of creation is the revolt of man against existing conditions, the aspiration of man to create life in his own image and to undergo a process of regeneration that does not stop for a single moment.[183]

The recognition of the unnatural and unwholesome state of existence in the Diaspora, he claimed, precedes the embarking upon a new life in Israel. The ills and evils of existing society must be diagnosed before the formula for another society can be drawn up. These, as-indicated, are both Jewish and human failings inherent in the environmental conditions. We witness "how poor, limited and narrow are human relationships in society, how little room there is for life of universal breadth and depth."[184] Similarly, the Jewish and the human factors are intertwined in the process of reconstruction. The inferior lot of the Jew-human being, caused not so much by the accident of fate as by the choice of environment and pursuit of livelihood, will be automatically and immeasurably improved in the rehabilitation of the individual. This, in turn, will lead to the remaking of society. Proletarianization and ruralization give rise to conditions that drastically reduce inter-human strife and, eventually, national hostilities. The new reality can approximate the cherished ideals of humanity. Gordon started with the condition of man and wound up with the state of society, without abandoning his initial emphasis on the individual.

> We must create a new nation, a human nation that has a brotherly human relationship toward other nations.[185]
>
> We must direct it toward the development of the human spirit, toward the search for truth and righteousness in its relationship with other peoples and with all mankind.[186]

Individual fulfillment in these social terms brings both inner peace and dynamic reorganization of the powers of personality. Man discovers a new and greater self as he escapes from his former selfishness.

> Here in infinite expanse everyone will find himself a wide course, as wide as the course of the sun and the stars. Here will the son of man be bound to his brother with celestial bonds.

> The primary reform that the life of labor in the midst of Nature institutes within man, is perfection . . . the perfect unity, the complete participation and unification of all the spiritual forces within him, in every aspect of life. Perception, emotion, instinct, physiological powers and physical powers of the body—all partake simultaneously and harmoniously . . . of the combined vastness of life.[187]

A remarkable philosophical formula embodying economic theories, national interests, psychological factors and spiritual-mystical values!

VII

Gordon's influence on the intellectual climate of Israel and the philosophy and curriculum of its educational system is profound. The axis of Land–Labor–Individual Fulfillment retains its pioneer attraction and pervades the public school, both secular and religious. The ideal in its three-fold aspect remains a moving force in the lives of large segments of youth as they make their homes in desert settlements and frontier outposts. Former Premier Ben Gurion personally dramatized this cause when he temporarily withdrew from government office in 1953 to become a shepherd in a southern desert colony.

In Gordon's universe of discourse, the only good teacher is the one who disproves the contention: "those who can, do; those who can't teach." He teaches by example, thereby communicating effectively with his students:

> The teacher as educator—if he really is prepared for his profession—must first of all be a philosopher with a full, individual world-outlook; that is, before he can educate man, he must know man; he cannot know man except through his own inner world. He must, too, be a son of

> nature, for his task is not alone to train man as a social and a national product, but primarily as a cosmic phenomenon, for as far as the pupil is concerned, his world is within himself . . . The educator must be the book or the living image, so that the student without will see and realize what the educator has created and creates of himself and of his talents.[188]

To Gordon, the process of self-education is the key to human progress. The panaceas of 'isms', the promises of ideologies, social reforms and political programs are secondary to man's re-education of himself. Final redemption is ushered in from within.

> Let the wise and practical men say what they will . . . Let all kinds of politicians, socialists, bring redemption to the world through the class struggle . . . Redemption will come to the world, rejuvenation to life, and salvation to man only through self-education as man is renewed by his very labor for the renewal of life in a human-cosmic brotherhood, and in the spiritual bond with all of life; and—above all—with the members of the community who labor for the renewal of life of a renewed people.[189]

It was Gordon's privilege to lay the foundation for a society that aspired to be model by remodeling himself and others in his orbit. His was an attempt to get the most out of life by practicing the highest human ideals in the service of his people.

The lines of a popular song in Israel, which is sung to the music of the national folk dance, the *Hora,* read: "We have come to the land to build and to be rebuilt." Nearly half a century after Gordon's death, the lyrics conveying the message of his teachings and his life, are still a "hit" in the parade of a nation on the march to a brighter future.

A JEWISH SOCIALIST SOCIETY

Nachman Syrkin

I

TWO IDEALS fired the imagination of Jewish youth at the turn of the 20th century, and continued to illuminate the path of Jewry in subsequent decades. Zionism and Socialism, commanding the loyalties of large segments of a rising intelligentsia and aroused masses, began at loggerheads with each other as the First World Zionist Congress in Basle and the Jewish Socialist *Bund* in Warsaw were both convened in 1897. The interaction and integration of these divergent ideas, along with the combination of these opposing forces, generated the power for the forging of the new state of Israel. National revival and social revolution were the two banners under which rallied the revolutionary forces of a persecuted people, the marching columns meeting on the horizon of a new dawn in the ancient homeland.

The dream was first expressed by Moses Hess in *Rome and Jerusalem* in the 1860's. The ideological structure was erected by Nachman Syrkin and Ber Borochov some forty years later, to combine nation and class, the economic and ethnic, materialistic and spiritual. Their ideological tracts and organizational leadership gave impetus to a movement which played a dominant role in the prenascent stage of Israel's destiny. Syrkin was a man of prophetic zeal and inspired vision, while Borochov was a profound thinker endowed with a scientific, analytic mind. The result was the synthesis of Socialist-Zionism, an ideology still championed by the controlling powers in the government of Israel and exerting a powerful influence on its social system.

Socialism and Zionism both sought an answer to the Jewish problem, each in its own way. Marxism, with its dialectical materialistic interpretation of history, ascribed the plight of Jews solely to the economic factor of capitalism. The socialists claimed that a proletarian society, cleansed of bourgeois classes, would remove the cause for national antagonisms and thus eliminate the discrimination against minorities. The Yiddish-speaking socialists of the *Bund*, distinguishable from their Jewish assimilationist companions, were beginning to advocate a separate but equal status for the Jewish proletariat which was to join forces with others in bringing about the world revolution. They were opposed to emigration, confident that the approaching era would bring relief to the Jewish masses in Eastern Europe without necessarily compelling them to shed their ethnic plummage. Deprecating nationalism as a regressive force, the *Bund* at first utilized Yiddish only as an internal vehicle of expression to expedite the class struggle. Later, it affirmed the innate value of Jewish group survival. Territorialism generally, and Zionism particularly, were regarded as unworthy sentimentalism, a desertion of the class struggle and an impediment to the wheels of revolution. In turn, Zionists deplored the hold of Marxist dogma over increasing numbers and the diversion of corporate energy from the promising front of national redemption to the arid field of social conflict. At the turn of the century universalistic socialism, together with assimilationism, even more than Marxism, emerged as the arch enemies of the Zionist movement.

II

Nachman Syrkin (Russia 1867-New York 1924) was the trailblazer who undertook and accomplished the synthesis between socialism and Zionism. Contemporaneous with the organization of the world Zionist movement, Syrkin, young leader of Russian Jewish emigres in Berlin, issued a treatise entitled *The Jewish Problem and the Jewish Socialist State*. In contrast to other Jewish socialists, he opposed assimilation. In this respect he was preceded by Chaim Zhitlowsky whose brochure expressing a similar viewpoint had appeared in 1892. But Zhitlowsky, who accepted nationalism in his socialist program, was not yet ready to embrace Zionism; while Syrkin, a committed Zionist, advocated a socialist state in Palestine as the only answer to the Jewish problem. His numerous journalistic efforts in Yiddish, German and Hebrew established him as the spokesman for the fledgling Socialist-Zionist *Poalei Zion* party. Thereafter, his intellectual influence and force of personality were deeply felt in Labor Zionist circles in Europe, Israel and America, the latter becoming his home for the last decade and a half of his life.

Syrkin approached nationalism and socialism from ethical premises. He believed that the same moral considerations of equality and freedom underlying socialism apply equally to nationalism. Any attempt to foster universalism at the expense of the interests of an ethnic group was a violation of socialist principles and inimical to true internationalism:

> The socialist movement staunchly supported all attempts of suppressed peoples to free themselves . . . the right of every nation to self-determination has consistently been proclaimed as an ideal organically related to the ethic of socialism.[190]

Syrkin believed that the socialist reconstruction of society was made necessary by the default of liberalism. The latter, originally dedicated to fostering freedom in its individual as well as national ramifications, had discarded its ideals in the struggle for economic power. Freedom of competition inevitably led to conflict, war and persecution of the Jews. Socialism, however, with its projected reshuffling of the economy and revamped social structure, would remove the cause for friction and oppression among civilized peoples and increase the opportunities for cultural intercourse, paving the way for true internationalism. A proper understanding of socialism, therefore, affirms the right and duty of the Jew to self-determination. This, so far, is the socialist basis for Jewish nationalism.

What about the *Jewish* motive for socialism? Syrkin claimed that the social revolution with its subsequent elimination of class conflict would destroy the basis for anti-Jewish bias, nourished as it had been by the ills of capitalist society. Self-interest, therefore, dictated to the Jew to join the ranks of the socially conscious proletariat which was aiming toward a new social order. Thus:

> The Jew has been the torchbearer of liberalism which emancipated him as part of its war against the old society; today after the liberal bourgeoisie has betrayed its principles and has compromised with those classes whose power

> rests on force, the Jew must enter the vanguard of socialism.[191]

Socialist and Jewish national goals merged on the Jewish scene and joined forces in the international class struggle.

Such rapproachment between Jewish nationalism and socialism was a novel and controversial idea at the turn of the century. Zionists regarded socialists with suspicion. Jewish socialists vehemently opposed the new movement. The assimilationist tendencies of the upper stratum of Jewish society were shared by the socialist intelligentsia who paraded under the banner of universalism. Syrkin's effort at a synthesis was an attempt to achieve within the Jewish camp what had already been developed among other European national minorities. Following contemporary examples, Syrkin called upon the socialists to become the standard-bearers of the Zionist movement. He believed that, inevitably

> Jewish socialism will, sooner or later, remove assimilatory tendencies from its ranks, and will openly declare itself to be the great protest movement of Jewry. As a protest movement against Jewish suffering, socialism can become the common possession of all Jews, because Jewish suffering affects every class of Jewry. . . .[192]

He thus envisaged a socialism embraced by non-proletarians as well, since it was designed to eradicate religious and racial persecution by removing the economic ills.

What was this socialism advocated by Syrkin in its operational context of Jewish national revival? He was not a Marxist. Admitting that "class struggle is the main driving force of history," he yet insisted that

> It is a misconception to explain all social life . . . in terms of this alone. All defensive, creative, and ideological ac-

> tivities are realized not through the class struggle but despite it.[193]

He affirmed spiritual values in his quest for economic reorganization of society, recognizing the historical aspirations of the Jewish people.

With regard to socialism's answer to the Jewish problem, Syrkin distinguished between long-range and immediate solutions. Unquestionably, the ultimate establishment of the new order could end discrimination, but that would be achieved in the remote future. The middle class status of the Jews and the absence of a large Jewish proletariat placed the Jewish group among those who would benefit least from the socialist upheaval. The economically unstable middle class merchants and professionals, the small tradesmen, peddlers and independent artisans of the lower class would have little to gain in the immediate aftermath of a social revolution. Consequently, emigration became for Syrkin the only solution. Palestine, as the historical homeland, was the logical haven. There, a new economic structure based on equalitarian and productive foundations inspired by Jewish idealism would avoid the evils of capitalist society.

> The guidelines of the new Jewish state must be justice, rational planning, and social solidarity. . . . The hope for a Messiah, always the basic sentiment of the Galut Jew, will be converted into political fact.[194]

Syrkin's conception of a Jewish state contained elements of the prophetic messianism of the Bible and Talmud, combined with modern political and economic theory. It was unaffected by Marxian dialectical materialism and the all-pervading revolutionary class struggle. It blended readily with romantic nationalism, marshaling the allegiance of idealistic youth inspired by Jewish historical experience and provoked by existing grim realities in Europe. He lashed out against the prevailing socialist rejection of basic Jewish self-interest, with the anomalous result that on

> numerous political occasions . . . the party rejoiced in anti-Semitism.[195]

He pleaded for human dignity to elicit self-acceptance through identification with Jewish national goals.

> The assimilated Jewish socialist, and on account of him, the non-Jewish socialist as well, regard the Jewish people as a means, a commodity of no value *per se,* except insofar as it serves the interests of others . . . (They) have not the courage to declare that since anti-Semitism is injurious to the Jew, they are obligated to combat it as Jews.[196]

A change of attitude toward their own people by Jewish socialists would also be reflected in their behavior toward the challenges of the non-Jewish environment, and particularly toward anti-Semitism. The result would be an increased stature which would prove of value in coping with the environment. Then would they fulfill "the dictate of our life, and the dictate of our honor, human and national."[197]

III

Syrkin's fusion of international socialism and Jewish nationalism was a pioneer venture, coming as it did in the formative years of the Zionist movement. In the immigrant student circles of Berlin, young Syrkin's dynamic personality and fervent espousal of these ideas exerted a decisive influence. The endless discussions on the nature of the

Jewish group and the solution of the Jewish problem were guided toward the development of a positive Jewish consciousness by the pathos and brilliance of Syrkin's elucidation. His brochure amplifying this thesis, *The Jewish Problem and the Jewish Socialist State,* appeared in 1898 only two years after Theodor Herzl's momentous little volume, *The Jewish State,* and one year after the world Zionist movement was launched by the first Zionist Congress. In the following decade, the seemingly novel ideas took root and blossomed forth into the ideological formulation of an organized party. They were further crystalized some twenty years later in a restatement attempted by Syrkin in a booklet published in 1917 entitled *National Independence and International Unity.**

In this essay the author surveyed the history of nationalism in its dichotomous role of a regenerative and abortive force. Nationalism has often contributed toward oppression, aiding the more powerful to despoil the weaker nation and impress its culture upon the subdued. Among those in command, nationalism is transformed into a reactionary power source used to defend the *status quo* and obstruct progressive change. The conquered, however, draw liberating and dynamic stamina from nationalism, reinforcing to human values and universal aspirations. Suppressed peoples express in their nationalism their quest for political freedom, group solidarity, cultural development, equity and equality among the family of nations. Syrkin felt that this type of nationalism characterized—or should characterize—Jewish socialism.

* The analysis of Syrkin's contributions are presented in chronological order. A systematic discussion of Syrkin's thought without regard to stages of development fails to take into account the impact of early theories in a particular historical setting. Syrkin's theories of 1898 may lack the depth and comprehensiveness of his mature thinking of 1917, but compensate for this in their originality and the epoch-making forces they set into motion.

> Nationalism has a dual meaning and diametrically opposite tendencies . . . To the ruling elements . . . suppression and negation of foreign nations, inflation of their own value, stagnation and petrification of national culture, and sanctification of traditions . . . The nationalism of oppressed elements is a recognition of the principle of equality . . . (seeing) in its own nation not only an end in itself but also an instrument for the good of humanity.[198]

Syrkin maintained that national entities have characters of their own. The national forms—through the culture—express the social and spiritual life of the people, refined and molded by the accumulated experience of ages. Each nation has a "mission" dictated by the historic sequence of events. "History has found its highest expression in the abundance of nations, and celebrates its triumph in the varieties and colors of the national cultures."[199] The highest types of national culture contain universal elements incorporated in the heritage of the human race. "Nationalism and internationalism, people and humanity, individualism and universalism are, in the final analysis, complementary terms."[200]

This has been the achievement of Judaism and of the Greek and Roman worlds. The Jews did not lose their authentic and distinct attributes when they were deprived of sovereignty and territory. The desire for national redemption, though sometimes dormant, was never dead throughout the dispersion. The rise of Zionism, reviving the zeal for national redemption, is a valid testimony to the vitality which still propels the Jewish people to heroic efforts at reconversion to a normal national existence. As such, they cannot be ignored by international socialism which, by the end of World War I "fully recognized the historical truth that each nation has a right and a duty to determine its own path in history."[201] As socialists abandon their naive belief in the cosmopolitan, homogeneous society they are also bound to accept the Jewish group.

National self-determination for the Jewish people entails the right to unhampered cultural life and communal organization. Zhitlowsky had already demonstrated this in the 90's, and the Jewish Socialist Bund accepted the idea after abandoning its initial anti-nationalistic position. Syrkin regarded this as a valuable palliative in the process of national self-determination. For a permanent cure, however, the measure of national self-determination granted to others—territorial independence—is the only prescription.

> There are two roads in the historical solution of the Jewish problem. First, the awakening of revolutionary political instincts of the Jewish masses, with the Jewish social democratic movement and the proletariat in the center, and the remaining groups in the periphery. Secondly, the redirection of the chaotic emigration of the eternally wandering Jews toward a territory, for the purpose of forming a Jewish State on socialist foundations. This territory is ancient Israel.[202]

Syrkin had great faith in the ability of the Jewish proletariat to achieve these goals. He was convinced that the spiritual forces revealed in Jewish history could be harnessed and directed toward the fulfillment of a greater destiny.

> A free country for the Jewish nation is not a contradiction, but the fulfillment of Jewish socialism. It is also the logical conclusion of Zionism that the independent Jewish homeland is to be built on higher social foundations . . . Whoever believes in the power of the Jewish nation, and whoever

> hopes for the revival of the Jewish people cannot conceive it without the leadership of the proletariat.[203]

IV

Syrkin's theories anticipated subsequent historical events. Jewish labor preceded Jewish capital in the reclamation of land and development of industry in Palestine. The unparalleled determining role of organized labor in Israel's economy today with its unchallenged leadership in government and society, is the actual realization of Syrkin's vision of a half century ago. His belief that there could be no possible improvement of Jewish life under a revolutionary regime in Russia has been tragically verified by the course of events which has remained unchanged to the present day.

Syrkin owed much to his predecessors. Moses Hess preceded him in the blending of socialist and Jewish national aspirations, which Syrkin freely admitted in his writings. Zhitlowsky's call for a return to Jewish cultural expression within the framework of socialism predated Syrkin's appearance. Others have been responsible for the actual unfolding of national and social reconstruction in the land of Israel. A. D. Gordon's idealism and personal practice had a greater impact on the emergence of Israel's social ideas and structure. Nevertheless, the theoretical formulation in the synthesis of non-Marxian socialism with nationalism in general and Zionism in particular, was Syrkin's leading contribution. It is interesting to note that Otto Bauer and other authoritative Central European intellectual leaders of socialism subsequently bridged the gap between socialism and nationalism, thereby giving, albeit indirectly, belated recognition to Syrkin's pioneer endeavor.

V

Like so many of the inspired personalities who shaped the movement that brought the State of Israel into being, Syrkin was a man of total commitment. His personal interests, economic status and family life were all subordinate to the demands of the idea that possessed him throughout his lifetime. As a result he was subject to conditions of instability and strain for many years—the frequent changes of residence and the uncertainty of earning even a meagre livelihood. In 1920, for example, he gave up the security of a weekly salary as a journalist for an established Yiddish daily in order to assume a less remunerative responsibility with the ephemeral organ of the party. That this course brought neither bitterness nor complaint is a tribute to his wife who was identified with Syrkin's vision early in their married life, and who chose to share whatever lot befell them. After she died of an illness aggravated by the conditions under which they lived, a younger sister arrived to take her place at his side in the pilgrimage.

Syrkin's last days were staged theatrically in the classical tradition. Free thinker though he had been, outspokenly anti-clerical, he yet chose to die as a religious Jew, abiding by the ritual requirements to the extent of offering confession in the presence of a rabbi. As in the case of so many avowed Jewish secularists with spiritual roots in the East European Jewish heritage, he had cherished fond sentiments for the traditional way of life by giving some expression to it in his own home. During Syrkin's final days in 1924 the New York Yiddish press dramatically reported his failing strength. He was mourned by the masses. But

> the true moment of memorial came twenty seven years later when Ben Gurion stepped out of the shadows on the shores of the Kinneret and vowed at the reinterment of Syrkin "Your vision shall be fulfilled".[204]

It was.

SYNTHESIS OF ZIONISM AND MARXISM

Ber Borochov

I

In 1966 an Israeli publishing house issued a volume of Ber Borochov's studies in Yiddish linguistics and literary history which originally appeared in various publications over a half century before.[205] This impressive, scholarly collection was published on the eve of the fiftieth anniversary of the death of its author, whose important research in Yiddish language and literature was overshadowed by his historical role as the brilliant theoretician of an ideology which exerted decisive influence in modern Jewish life and thought.

Little known in intellectual circles in the United States, the name of Ber Borochov (Russia, 1881-1917) continues to evoke reverence and devotion in an important segment of Israel society and elsewhere throughout the Jewish world. To a degree he was for some, in his day, what Maimonides was for others in *his* day—a synthesis between the Jewish commitment and the intellectual challenge of the age. In the instance of Maimonides, it was Jewish tradition versus Greek philosophy. For the generation of Ber Borochov, it was Jewish nationalism versus Marxist dogma. Borochov's historical achievement was the theoretical fusion of the two by a thorough, analytical reconciliation of Marxist dialectical materialism and Zionist idealistic aspirations.

The Socialist-Zionist movement, which played the major role in the upbuilding of Israel, owes its origin to Nachman Syrkin and Ber Borochov who appeared on the Jewish horizon at about the turn of the century. Both erected ideological structures, housing under one roof socialist principles with Zionist goals. Syrkin burst forth on the national stage a year after the launching of the Zionist movement by Theodor Herzl in 1897. Borochov appeared on the scene five years later.

As previously indicated, the Socialist-Zionist dream first fired the imagination of Moses Hess during the early 1860's. Some three decades later Chaim Zhitlovsky attempted to close the gap between socialism and nationalism, exerting an influence on many intellectuals. In the subsequent decade the ideological structure was completed by Syrkin and Borochov. They became the spiritual and organizational architects of the movement which laid the foundation for state and society in Israel. Syrkin, a disciple of the non-Marxian idealistic school of socialism, was bolstered by the inspiration and zeal for social justice drawn from the prophets of ancient Israel. Just a few years later, Ber Borochov was eminently successful in applying Marxist dogma to the Jewish problem, and arriving at a Zionist solution within the framework of socialist doctrine.

Within a relatively short but creative life, Borochov constructed an edifice of ideas which proved of sufficient magnitude to reach beyond the Jewish intellectual horizon. Borochovism became a platform of an organized

Jewish political party, as well as an official designation of a program adopted by non-Jewish socialists in the Ukraine. Like Syrkin, his field of operation encompassed Eastern and Central Europe, with a limited span of activity in the United States. In the capacity of spokesman for Socialist Zionism, he revisited Russia after the Revolution. It was during this sojourn that sudden illness led to his untimely death. He was one of the two founding fathers of Zionism in the twentieth century who had never set foot in Palestine.

II

Borochov's doctrine was the first successful marriage of nationalism and dialectical materialism. He coined new terms to accomplish this task, such as "conditions of production" and "stychic process" to interpret historical and sociological phenomena. The result was a system of thought embracing nationalism generally, with its Jewish expression in Zionism set neatly within the firm hold of Marxian dialectics. An important, though decreasing segment of Israel's labor movement still adheres to the initial Borochov doctrine.

Borochov applied Marx's explanation of the class struggle to the national problem which had set Europe in turmoil in the last century. Marx had pointed to the clash between the *forces* of production represented essentially by labor as the real producers and the existing *relations* of production, which are the contrivances of legal ownership. Borochov added that the *forces* of production within a national unit come into conflict with the *conditions* of production in that national setting, the latter including geographic and historic factors impinging upon the interests of other national groups.

> The conditions of production . . . are geographic, anthropological and historic. The historic conditions include both those generated within a given social entity and those imposed by the neighboring social groups.[206]

As a society develops, the social and historical conditions of production assume a greater importance than the natural conditions. "This feeling of kinship, created as a result of the visioned common historic past and rooted in the common conditions of production is called nationalism."[207] It supplies the base for group effort directed toward attainment of territorial goals conducive to commonly shared material interests and collective welfare. In other words, the national and the economic interests merge.

Thus Borochov offered a purely materialistic approach to the national question. Just as class conflict is conducted not for intangibles, but for the means of production, *i.e.,* "the material possessions of the classes, so too, with the national struggle."[208]

But nationalism is not the same for all economic strata. It differs in content from upper to lower classes. For the landed aristocracy, the territory is valuable in terms of income it supplies. The bourgeoisie considers the territory home-plate for playing the commercial field. The middle class regards it as a market for consumer goods and is therefore interested in a unifying language and culture. For the proletariat, too, the national territory assumes special significance as the location for its own economic interests.

> One should not accept the wide-spread misconception in believing that the proletariat supposedly has no connection with the national territory and has, therefore, no national

> sentiments. . . . The territory is valuable to the proletariat as the work center.[209]

This is its initial function. Furthermore, the territory serves as the "strategic base" for conducting the class struggle. The national sovereign territory, supplying the base of operations for releasing the social forces engaged in economic conflict, becomes the indispensable setting for the ultimate triumph of socialism.

Borochov parallels Syrkin's concept of the divergent role of nationalism among dominating and dominated nations. In the former instance it is reactionary, obscuring the class struggle in the desire for expansion at the expense of other nations, and requires in its course the collaboration of all classes. In the latter situation there is a true convergence of class and national interests—the striving of a subjugated people to eliminate foreign control if its territory satisfies the objective of the proletariat to establish a strategic base for the class struggle. This is possible only in the free interplay of economic forces, unhampered by overbearing outside control. The nationalism of a suppressed nation becomes a prerequisite in preparation for the emerging class struggle. The drive for national independence is then conducive to socialist goals and consistent with Marxist principles. Borochov achieves a remarkable synthesis in bridging the gap between heretofore mutually exclusive ideologies!

Borochov further distinguishes between types of nationalism along historical lines, as nationalism changes its function with the advent of modern times. The nationalism of oppressed peoples, in the age of capitalism, is an authentic expression of historic forces which set the stage for the proletarian revolution.

Abnormal and lamentable is the lot of Jewish labor in

the crucible of nationalism and class conflict. The Jewish workers, unlike the native inhabitants, belong to a landless nation and suffer a double disability, both as Jews and proletarians. Regarded as foreigners in their various domiciles, they are expelled from primary economic pursuits (agriculture, heavy industry) and by necessity are compelled to enter secondary occupations (commerce, light industry, white collar). This in itself places them in a less advantageous position *vis-à-vis* the class struggle which is conducted largely from the base of essential ("primary") industries.

In further stages of development, the native population begins to compete with the Jewish merchant, professional, and wage-earner of the "secondary" level, with the result that the Jewish minority is encroached upon in its own remaining economic pursuits. Thus the Jewish group is initially relegated to less productive areas, and subsequently subjected to repressive competition. On account of the diminishing value of its services to the economic system, the members of the Jewish proletariat are prevented from playing their proper social and political roles in the class struggle. Inevitably under pressure from the majority, they are forced to emigrate and seek a livelihood in new lands.

There the cycle begins again in the sequence of economic development from primitive to advanced stages of commercial enterprise and technological activity in the rise and eventual demise of capitalism.

> We are aliens and nowhere in the world do we have the power to control our own condition . . . Our history in exile was never molded by our own strength. Our fate was always dependent on outside factors. Can the rapid pace of progress redeem us from this state of uprootedness and insecurity?[210]

Borochov answered in the negative. From the point of view of dialectical materialism this is an inescapable process. Therefore Jews must eventually settle in an undeveloped country such as Palestine, where the indigenous population is small enough to allow for large Jewish colonization without the immediate threat of clashing economic interests.

Through territorial concentration and the emergence of a Jewish majority, the Jewish problem reaches a solution—since the Jewish proletariat is then free to enter agriculture and basic (primary) industry, retaining thereby independent control of the conditions of production. No longer is it at the mercy of others. The new home passes through the various stages of capitalistic development and becomes ripe for social revolution generated and directed by the Jewish proletariat. In Palestine, therefore "Jewish migration must be transformed from immigration into colonization."[211] The majority Jewish population utilizes the homeland as a strategic base for the class struggle, leading to the realization of Zionism simultaneous with the attainment of socialism. This he termed a "stychic" process, inferring that it is inherent in the very course of history as existing and evolving conditions assume their logical and natural sequence.

But why only Palestine as a base of operations? Borochovs' reply is that Palestine is the most feasible territory for the realization of socialism. There, a Jewish proletariat can flourish under normal conditions in the struggle for the new order. Palestine fulfills the required stipulations by virtue of being "not close to a cultural center, on the sea-coast, and having a nomadic population" numerically limited.[212] The difficulty of acclimatization for Europeans and the paucity of natural resources make it unattractive to non-Jewish westerners. Jewish capital and labor, both at a disadvantage in the lands of their origin, gravitate to Palestine where they confront each other in a setting under their own control.

> The Jewish worker comes to Palestine with his proletarian revolutionary class consciousness and experience in the class struggle . . . The Jewish entrepreneur who comes to settle has had similar experience.[213]

In the new arena latent productive energy is released and channelled into class conflict, as the Jewish proletariat "improves its strategic base."

Palestine then provides relief for the economic difficulties of the Jewish masses. Concomitantly, other traumas of the Jewish condition are eliminated. Social and political disability, psychological insecurity and problems of national geographic diffusion are mitigated. "Zionism is the only movement capable of introducing reason, order and discipline into Jewish life. (It) is the only answer to the economic and historic need of the Jewish people."[214]

The automatic unfolding of these stages in Borochov's "stychic process"—economic displacement, emigration, colonization of Palestine, transplanted class struggle, and finally the social revolution—requires a catalyst to accelerate the tempo. The active aid of human effort is often necessary in order for the historical tendencies to be realized in reasonable time.

> Along with the stychic social tendencies, we must inject into the process a conscious tendency. . . . The conscious interference cannot create and improvise stychic processes, but only regulate them, that is, facilitate and accelerate their pace.[215]

The logical conclusion establishes the need for an organized Zionist Socialist movement to expedite and reinforce the historical processes. The dogma of socialist Marxism has thus been transformed by an analytical *tour de force* into a philosophy of Zionism.

III

Borochov perceived in nationalism a force for human dignity enabling the Jew to rise in stature and attain self-respect in spite of a social climate making for his humiliation. He went so far as to declare: "We must understand once and for all that one who has no national dignity has no class dignity"[216]—in bold defiance of the multitude of assimilated Jewish radicals who let their Jewish identification evaporate. He challenged the *Bund,* the non-territorialist socialist nationalists (exponents of an *ad hoc* national program without emigration), on their deceptive reliance on the wheels of progress, which would eventually eliminate anti-Jewish discrimination:

> And they promise us and themselves victory over the reactionaries . . . But we Jews dare not wait. And we Zionists cannot wait . . . It is our deep conviction that there is no help for the Jewish people within the framework of exile. We do not rely on progress. . . . Progress is a great factor in the accelerated development of technology, science, and possibly even of the fine arts, but ethical advancement is still too remote.[217]

At a later period in his life, shortly before his sudden passing, Borochov attempted a reformulation of his views. Modifying his Marxian dialectics, he found room in his theoretical system for Jewish historical aspirations as a basis for Socialist Zionism. "We 'historical materialists' cannot completely ignore the past, especially when it involves the formation of a national ideal."[218] Initially he had justified the settlement of Palestine "by the force of historical necessity."[219] In his final address, however, he allowed himself some "emotional terminology" proclaiming, "The Land of Israel—a Jewish home."[220]

These sprouting deviations from Marxist dogmatism might have reached fuller blossom if Borochov's life had not been cut short so prematurely. After the outbreak of the Russian Revolution, Borochov, like so many other socialists, was captivated by its messianic phraseology and he hurried back from his two year sojourn in the United States to witness and participate in the building of the new society. In the midst of devoted over-activity he contracted pneumonia and died shortly thereafter at the age of thirty-six.

Committed to the Zionist solution as dialectically inevitable in the course of events, Borochov did not advocate nor necessarily envisage the ingathering of *all* Jews into Palestine. He recognized that there would always remain large segments of Jewry throughout the world. Though Palestine's absorption of increasing numbers will offer a great relief to the displaced proletariat, an *ad hoc* constructive program is needed to protect world-wide Jewish interests outside of Palestine.

> Zionism solves only some of the Jewish problems, namely, homelessness and landlessness. . . . No matter to what extent Zionism is realized, there will always remain—possibly a majority—dispersed among other nations.[221]

A far-reaching and encompassing organizational platform was evolved for the home front. It was directed toward the economic, the communal and the cultural problems. As a result, Labor Zionism became a potent force in Jewish life. Its socialist ideology brought it into close partnership and official identification with the labor movements in various countries and with the political and economic aims of the Second Socialist International. On the local level, it fostered the organization of democratically representative Jewish communal agencies, embracing all areas of Jewish endeavor. Identification with the Jewish proletariat led to an appreciation of the folk tongue of the masses—the Yiddish language—the organization of schools, press and other media of cultural expression.

Borochov had championed Yiddish, and, although it was not his mother tongue, he made valuable and scholarly contributions to Yiddish philology, bibliography, folklore and literary history.

The many-faceted program for Jewish life throughout the world did not mitigate Labor Zionist efforts in behalf of Palestine. The major impetus for the colonization of the Land of Israel came from the ranks of Labor Zionism. In theory and practice it was all–encompassing, aimed at the reconstruction and revitalization of Jewish life wherever it is found and the establishment of a new society in the ancient homeland.

IV

Syrkin and Borochov were the recognized theoreticians and leaders of the ideological sector within Jewry which, over the years, offered the greatest intellectual ferment, creative activity and constructive achievements for the emergence of the Jewish State and the new Jewish society in Israel. They not only dealt with contemporaneous Jewish realities, but projected future conditions and outlined relevant provisions both for Israel and Jews abroad. A comparison of their fundamental views is therefore in order.

Syrkin, who drew his inspiration from ancient Jewish sources, accepted socialism only in its idealistic foundations and in some of its pragmatic conclusions without its materialistic philosophy of history. Borochov adopted Marxism and extended its economic determinism to embrace Jewish national goals. Syrkin, in contrast to Borochov, espoused the primacy of Hebrew both in Israel society and world Jewry. The "affirmation of Diaspora" viewpoint within the Zionist program, which posited continued Jewish life throughout the world even after the eventual fulfillment of the Zionist vision (in contrast to the "negation of Diaspora" concept) and called for constructive communal and cultural action on the local scene, gained its impetus more from Borochov than from Syrkin.

Yet it was Borochov's economic interpretation of history that compelled him never to deviate from the one logical territorial goal, namely, Palestine. Over a number of years, Syrkin the non-Marxist, allowed himself to flirt with non-Zionist territorialism which sought to find a homeland other than Palestine for the Jewish people. The impact of Borochov's thought was felt by large numbers of Jewish intellectuals who espoused the economic determinism of Marx and his disciples. Cultural, spiritual and historical arguments in behalf of Zionist aspirations would have made little impression on them. During the early half of the first decade of the twentieth century, when the British African territory of Uganda was dangled before the Jewish masses, the socialist sector of Zionism would have proved most susceptible to the temptation if it were not for Borochov's utilization of Marxist dialectics to prove that Israel was the only choice for the Jews in the perspective of historical materialism.

In the course of world events and Jewish realities,

Syrkin's idealism seemed to be more consonant with the changing times. While both have exerted a profound influence on Israel society, current Israel social thought is more indebted to Syrkin's idealistic socialism than to Borochov's dialectical materialism. For decades class consciousness in the spirit of Borochov had been fostered by labor groups in Palestine, particularly in the agricultural and industrial collectives. However, after the establishment of the State in 1948 it became evident that Marxist political orientation, class struggle and activism had run their full course.

Unlike the American trade-union movement, organized labor in Israel has been articulately socialistic; its Borochov-oriented segment has been ostensibly Marxist. Israel economy, more a creation of organized labor and world Jewish philanthropy than of private capital, has established a planned economy and developed a socialist society-within-a-society in the plethora of industrial plants, commercial and agricultural enterprises launched and managed by organized labor. The Yugoslav system of shared profits by workers is operative in the majority of agricultural establishments and in a number of industrial units. But the numerous factories and social services, founded and operated by the labor movement, are under centralized control of the *Histadrut*; the stresses and strains, profits and losses of the various manufacturing and commercial enterprises balance each other to preserve and foster a pioneer but growing economy. A voluntary type of socialist society within the framework of a democratic state has emerged without infringing to any considerable extent upon the operations of private capital. Socialism, as a doctrine, is still espoused, and the first of May is a widely observed labor holiday. But for the majority of workers it is more in the spirit of Syrkin's non-Marxist socialism with its inspired experimental idealism, than of Borochov's early dogmatism with its dialectic materialistic context. The banner raised by the two founders of Labor Zionism is held high by Israel labor and intelligentsia, instrumental in determining the future of the infant state and influencing the destiny of an ancient people far beyond Israel's borders.

Borochov's doctrine prevails in leftist socialist circles—the *Achdut Avodah** and *Mapam* parties—the latter equating progress with the oncoming New Order and "wave of tomorrow" of the Soviet world, though Russia vehemently rebuffs any overtures from this Israeli sector. Yet Marxist dogmatism is still applied to areas beyond the economic, such as in historical studies, literary and art criticism and social research.

Borochov's early revolutionary militancy still expresses the contemporary mood of at least one Labor Zionist party:

> The working class raises the pillar of fire of the new truth and the new culture . . . its own philosophy, ethics, science and art in new forms and a new spirit . . . (It is) a proletarian culture.[222]

On the other hand, Syrkin's spirit, to a degree, dominated the policies of the *Mapai,* which represented the majority of Israel labor and has been the party in power since the inception of the State. Its social experimentation, political flexibility and national maturity (occasionally at the expense of narrow class interest for the sake of national survival) bespeak the responsibility and vision necessary in the maelstrom of world events, colored by a characteristically Jewish social idealism.

* In 1968, a merger was effected between the small *Achdut Avoda* and the large centre party *Mapai* to form *Avoda.*

> Above all social, economic, material motives of Zionism, there hovers the idealistic motive emanating from the depth of the human soul returning to it in a beckoning creative form.[223]

Israel education is a case in point. Socialism was the official philosophy of the labor schools until their dissolution in 1953 by a labor government. Yet, Borochov's ideas are still popular among teachers in some of the collective colonies. The transfer "from class to nation" (the title of a book by former Premier Ben Gurion) is accepted by most educators formerly associated with the labor schools. The public schools had been removed from party control in 1953. Western sophistication is bringing maturity to a community previously addicted to ideologies, while the idealism, vision and values of the pioneer generation retain their pristine appeal, potency and cogency in the midst of the atomic age. The formation of new border *kibbutzim*, after the Six Day War of June, 1967, transplanting young people to frontier settlements in Sinai, the West Bank and the Golan Heights, is a testimony to the continued power of these ideals and to the caliber of the younger generation.

RELIGIOUS REBIRTH

Abraham Isaac Kuk

I

Zionism, viewed in historical perspective, is to be regarded as a factor for both continuity and change in the course of national events. Pioneers of Zionist thought have alternated between conservation and revolution, as the leitmotifs of their intellectual speculations on the Jewish problem. The formulators of the Zionist thesis were either strangers from afar, such as Hess and Herzl, who arrived with new ideas, or rebels from within like A. D. Gordon and Brenner, who set out toward new horizons. In their combined efforts they attracted generally the peripheral elements consisting of the secular, both idealistic and disillusioned, who had already been liberated, wholly or partially, from the confinement of the ghetto. The Orthodox masses, subject to the ritualistic regimen and mental discipline of the erudite and uncompromising rabbinate, hardly felt the positive impact of the Zionist movement. If anything, Orthodoxy responded with suspicion and opposition to the national ideal. Only a handful of recognized rabbis were favorably inclined toward Zionism at its inception, and some were among its founders, Among the latter were Zvi Kalisher of Prussia (d. 1874), Mordecai Eliasberg of Latvia (d. 1889) , the Sfardi rabbi of Serbia, Yehudah Alkalai (d. 1869), and especially Samuel Mohliver of Poland (d. 1898). Although highly regarded in their own communities, these were not the key figures, the most revered authorities and sages of renown throughout the Jewish world. The most eminent rabbis with the widest following remained aloof and often antagonistic toward the new movement.

It was Abraham Isaac Kuk, Chief Rabbi of Palestine, who commanded the esteem necessary for a successful and fruitful fusion of Orthodoxy and Zionism, developing a philosophy firmly rooted in the religious heritage, while simultaneously embracing the nationalistic program in complete consonance with it. He elevated religious Zionism to spiritual heights in the perspective of continuity, charging it with the power to galvanize large segments of traditional Jewry in behalf of the reclamation of the ancient homeland. Without negating the political, cultural and economic ideas of the secular-minded theorists of Zionism, he set them into a religious framework in perfect blending of contemporary and traditional values. This was an undertaking of singular importance, bridging the gulf between embattled forces, each jealously guarding its own domain. The accomplishment was made possible by a fortunate combination of circumstances insofar as a saintly personality was placed in the exalted central position of Chief Rabbi of Palestine, and an original mind was engaged in creative deliberations which produced literary works of lasting spiritual value.

Retrospectively, the Orthodox position *vis-à-vis* Zionism is best comprehended in the light of education in Israel today. The unified school system includes a network of government-supported religious schools, catering to a substantial minority of the population. These schools combine a general education with training in the observance of ritual and in the transmitting of the religious tradition. Not all like-minded parents enroll their children in these schools. The ultra-Orthodox element, comprising about 35,000 pupils, is in the *Chinuch Atzmai* ("Independent Education") system which receives limited financial backing from the government. These differ, not in ritual practice, but in the attitude toward educational and national values cultivated in the public schools. In the past, Zionism was anathema to this group, though since the birth of the State it is no longer a moot issue. Co-education, along with much that pervades the modern curriculum, has been unpalatable to the "Independent" backers.

The Israeli education picture, therefore, includes the general public school and two parallel religious school systems, one public and one semi-private. The last two are distinguishable from each other more by their respective attitudes to the secular environment of state and society than by loyalty to particular religious dogma or adherence to ritual requirements. There is a tradition of competition and even hostility among their sponsors and originators, which goes back to the time when Zionism was a controversial issue. The "Independent" system aims to approximate the East European traditional school, unchanged for centuries. It is under the auspices of the separatist *Agudat Israel* ("Union of Israel"), an Orthodox party founded before World War I in opposition to Zionism.

The overwhelming majority of the religious population subscribes to a program which is a synthesis of Orthodoxy and modern nationalism, a philosophy reflected in the government-sponsored religious school. Its forerunner was the school system launched by the *Mizrachi*, the Orthodox wing of the Zionist movement, organized in 1902. Over the decades it succeeded in gaining the loyalty of increasing numbers among the Orthodox masses of Europe and America. The prevailing sentiment in Eastern Europe, however, was unsympathetic to political Zionism in the communities controlled by conservative rabbinical authorities. The acclaimed spiritual leader of religious nationalism, whose influence reached the entire community of Palestine, was Chief Rabbi Kuk.

Understanding more fully the ultra-Orthodox position would facilitate an appreciation of Rabbi Kuk's signal contribution.

Political Zionism, launched by Herzl at the end of the 19th century, ignited the spirit of the Jewish masses, but received a cool reception from rabbinical authorities. The entrenched religious officialdom was opposed to Zionism on psychological, theological and practical grounds. There was an inherited intransigence toward all new movements of messianic pretensions since historical antecedents had resulted in the formation of heretic sects, some of which actually seceded from Judaism. There was also a measure of inertia and stagnation which automatically rejected anything new and unfamiliar, particularly—as in the case of Zionism—when it suggested a departure from a two thousand year pattern of survival. Existing leadership and vested interests were suspicious of the new elements that were advancing to the forefront, mostly from non-conformist quarters. The traditional theology was committed to patient anticipation of the Messiah, "even though he tarry," instead of independent initiative directed toward immediate redemption from Exile, derisively dubbed "to force the End". Restoration of statehood through human instrumentalities and natural forces was tantamount to blasphemy. In Palestine, the "old settlement" centered in Jerusalem and the other "Holy Cities" (Hebron, Tiberias and Safed) objected to the productive economic mode of life advocated by the new settlers, who challenged the prevailing reliance upon charity from abroad. A vicious circle was thus created: Orthodoxy opposed Zionist colonization, leading to a predominance of liberal young people among the new arrivals who, in turn, antagonized Orthodoxy by their secular mode of living. Added to this was the transvaluation of Jewish life contained in the Zionist program, fostering a new outlook on physical work, economic enterprise, and cultural and social values, all in conflict with the inherited attitudes and accommodations. To cite one example among many, spoken Hebrew was regarded as an outright desecration by traditionalists who revered it as a holy tongue designed exclusively for sacred usage. Though not all rabbis were averse to the new outlook in its entirety, many of the great sages dwelling in isolation, as well as the articulate spokesmen for the traditional camp, reflected this antagonism in word and deed. In contrast, the saintly qualities and spiritual stature of Rabbi Kuk were instrumental in fostering a religious Zionism, merging religious orthodoxy with political nationalism into a dynamic and creative force for the rejuvenation of the Jewish people on its own soil, and the establishment of the State of Israel.

II

Abraham Isaac Kuk was born in Latvia in 1865. He was recognized as a prodigy and ordained at an early age. His studies included not only the jurisprudence of the Talmud but also the mystic lore of the Kabbalah as well as secular knowledge, the latter severely frowned upon in traditional quarters. The curriculum, unusual for those times, did not detract from his faith and piety. After serving a number of communities, he accepted a call to Jaffa, Palestine, arriving there in 1904. Except for the interlude of war years, during which he found himself stranded in Europe temporarily occupying a pulpit in London, Kuk lived in Palestine until his passing in 1935. After 1919, he held the exalted position of Chief Rabbi of the Ashkenazi community (European), the Sfardi congregations having their own Chief Rabbi (a historical division created by the varying traditions of ritual and religio-ethnic culture).

In his student years, Kuk came under the influence of the *Mussar* (Ethics) movement, founded by Israel Salanter—a religious revival aimed at moral perfection through introspection, austerity and discipline. Zionism was then in its embryonic stage. In the famed rabbinical seminary at Volozhin, Russia, which Kuk attended, he participated in a newly organized secret Zionist society. It was the Zionist motive which subsequently moved him to accept a post in the Holy Land in spite of the pressures brought to bear against depriving Russian Jewry of his spiritual leadership. In the meantime, he had blossomed forth into a great scholar and sage, a revered personality, esteemed at home and abroad. He had also taken up the pen to popularize his Zionist ideas, and to work out an original and all-pervasive philosophy of religious Zionism.

III

In one of his first essays, "The Mission of Israel and Its Nationhood" which appeared in 1901, Kuk sees no conflict between nationalism and religion. They are complementary to each other, each insufficient in itself. Jewish nationalism in its various forms of expression is indispensable for the survival and revival of Judaism. "We are to regard with approval all manifestations of the national spirit of the Jewish people."[224] Jewish nationalism, to Kuk, is not a secular force as misjudged by most of his contemporary rabbinical authorities. In spite of its modern and secular trappings, its foundations are in the spiritual heritage of the Jewish people. "The national sentiment", he maintained, "is holy and exalted in itself."[225] It is actually "the very foundation of Judaism, and essential to it."[226] For nationhood, his argument continues, was always an integral part of Jewish religion. Its fountainhead fed the streams of Jewish consciousness whenever the sources of piety were depleted. Thus, the nationalistic motif would induce Jewish loyalties when religious inspiration weakened.

Unfortunately, throughout its long trek, the Jewish people lost some of its national attributes and sentiments, becoming spiritually the poorer for it. Kuk, therefore, deplores "the lack of national feeling within us," and points to it as "a great and noble natural force, conducive to lofty perfection."[227]

Nationalism generally, and not only its Jewish form, is a positive force, generating spiritual progress. "It is impossible to reach a condition of moral perfection without the wholehearted love of one's nation."[228] The rise of nationalism is to be hailed as a significant stride in the history of man:

> Now that national sentiment has been aroused, nationalism has become a natural feeling, acquiring a rightful position in the development of mankind; our people, too, has benefited from it. . . . We must make every effort to reinforce it, to define and spell out its noble purpose among our people.[229]

Kuk was convinced that in his day an opportunity for replenishing Jewish spiritual strength had become available in the upsurge of national sentiment. The Jewish people could thereby share the potentialities for human and moral advancement with which Zionism is fraught. It follows, therefore, that religion has little to lose and much to gain by accepting the new nationalism within its fold.

The nature of Jewish peoplehood established optimum conditions for the permanent effects of the new force. Kuk affirms that Israel has fused a union between physical kinship and lofty idealism. The Divine has endowed the union with a holiness contingent upon the preservation of this state. This was a unique contribution of the Jewish genius. The task begun by Judaism at the dawn of history has not been completed. Recreating the original setting within the confines of the Holy Land paves the way for finishing the job.

> The inner feeling, so strong within us, in striving for the preservation of Judaism in its . . . corporal and territorial aspects, flows from the general public recognition that there is still much to be finished in what we have begun. We began to say something important to ourselves and the world, and we have not concluded it yet.[230]

> The spirit of the people restored by its return to the homeland, will make manifest its ancient qualities and the prophetic spirit in its Divine glory will emerge from its concealment.[231]

Thus, Jewish nationalism is elevated to universal significance.

To Kuk, deeply attached to his faith in all its depth and potency, the universal message of messianic Zionism was not a beautiful, poetic phrase to be bandied about indiscriminately. To him, it was to be taken not only seriously but literally. Its fulfilment was inevitable. Mystic that he was, he ascribed an innate sanctity to the people of Israel, charging the Biblical concept of a "holy people" with deepened and tangible meaning relevant to the entire Jewish community.

> The community of Israel is the essence of all existence. In this world, the essence flows directly into the Israelite nation; into its materiality no less than its spirituality; into its history no less than into its faith.[232]

The Zionist movement is not merely a humanitarian undertaking designed to create a haven of refuge for homeless wanderers. To Kuk, Zionism draws from the springs of Divine inspiration. It is an unfolding of a pre-determined eternal pattern of *a cosmic process* operating in history.

> The source of Zionism is that supreme sacred source, the Holy Writ, which imparts to it the depth and glory of tradition. It is fitting that we restore this eternal movement to life. Zionism is not the response of a people hated in the world, setting out to find for itself a refuge from its persecutors. Rather is it the fact that a Holy Nation, the choicest of peoples, the lion-cub of Judah, is awakening from its long sleep and is returning to its rightful habitat.[233]

The surface appearance of enthusiastic chauvinism notwithstanding, Kuk's love for humanity was unparalleled in its universal encompassment. In the manner of the medieval Jewish philosopher, Yehuda Halevi, he attributed an inherent sanctity to the soil of the Holy Land and the soul of the people. Palestine stamps its imprint upon all that occurs there, penetrating and far reaching in spiritual consequences. The beneficent effects are indirectly enjoyed by all men, as the spiritual forces released in the Holy Land are channeled into the turbines of cosmic power propelling human destiny.

> It is impossible to grasp the essence of the unique holiness of the land of Israel . . . by any rational human effort. The Divine Spirit in the nation at large, the inherent spiritual stamp of the soul of Israel generates rays in varying colors through all facets of experience in nature.[234]

Furthermore, the effect of the Holy Spirit absorbed in the land of Israel remains operative even when one leaves the land involuntarily.

IV

The Zionist formula, for its universal as well as national benefits, follows logically on these premises of Kuk. The benefits of Judaism accruing to the Jewish people and the nations of the world are best generated when the Jewish people flourishes in the Holy Land. Israel, the people and the land reunited, is a blessing to itself and mankind. Living in Israel is therefore a privilege in tune with a universal melody and in keeping with the Divine Will. To deprive oneself of this spiritual opportunity is an act of delinquency. It is a "sin for Israel to continue to dwell in the Diaspora." Kuk alone, among Orthodox rabbis, could see only good in secularly oriented young people who were dedicated to the upbuilding of the Land of Israel; and he responded to them with tolerance and love, which they appreciated and reciprocated.

The difference between the life of the spirit in Israel, and that of other lands, is the distance between two realms of existence.

> There is a profound difference between the Torah of Israel and the Torah of the Diaspora. In Israel, the Holy Spirit bursts forth on every scholar engaged in the study of the Torah per se . . . It is impossible to breathe the air of sanctity in an atmosphere of defilement in another land.[235]

The author maintans that he himself could testify to this fact. As a mystic, he experienced personally that which he articulated frequently in word and script. His fervent piety and profound mysticism nourished his nationalism. Yet, as already indicated, in his mystic nationalism he steered clear of narrow particularistic tendencies. The idea of munificent blessings to mankind, to be realized by Israel redeemed, was pivotal in his philosophy. Kuk's own horizon encircled all of humanity, and his heart throbbed with a genuine love for all nations.

> I love all. I cannot help loving individuals, all peoples. From the bottom of my being, I wish the glory of all, the perfection of all. My love for Israel is deeper and more glowing, but my inner wish spreads the might of my love over all. I do not have to force myself to this feeling of love; it issues directly from the sacred depth of wisdom, from the divine soul.[236]

Thus a sense of loyal and dedicated world citizenship emerges from a powerful but elevated attachment to ethnic aspirations.

V

Much of Kuk's voluminous writing was published posthumously. It is mystical, poetic and inspirational, considerably removed from the universe of discourse of the modern reader in Israel. Yet, his influence was profound, as much through his life as through his writing. He belonged to the intellectual pioneers who established the spiritual foundations for Zionism.

The author of an extensive work on the life and thought of the former Chief Rabbi of Palestine, calls attention to:

> elements in Kuk's thought that most discriminating readers will find unacceptable and even repugnant . . . conceptions which he took over bodily from Halevi and Kabbalah. These elements, however, are logically separated from the rest of his thoughts, which are of permanent value and universal human appeal.[237]

Rabbi Kuk exerted a powerful influence on a large segment of religious Jewry, on its network of schools and colonies. To a lesser, though not inconsequential degree, he reached into secular circles. He contributed toward a broader understanding of nationalism and a deeper religious insight, united in a religious Zionist synthesis.

What Syrkin and Borochov did for socialism and Marxism, Kuk accomplished for traditional Judaism—in closing the gap with Zionism. A contemporary of the architects of the Zionist structure and yet surviving them all, he incorporated their emphasis in his all-inclusive philosophy: the political goals of Herzl, the Hebrew language revival of Ben Yehuda, the spiritual aspirations of Ahad Ha'am, the sanctity of labor as propounded by A. D. Gordon, the social justice and social utopian aims of Syrkin and Borochov. He embodied all of these elements in his reinterpretation of Judaism and reformulation of Zionism, casting them together in a religious mold. And he dedicated his life to the fulfillment of these aims. The exalted position of the Chief Rabbinate was not utilized by Kuk for placing himself above the exigencies of the day. He involved himself in the concerns of his generation and faced forthrightly the issues dividing the community. He had the courage to justify, from a religious viewpoint, the right of labor to strike, and he refrained from castigating the *Chalutzim* who rejected outright all ritual sancta. He regarded them charitably as tillers in the vineyard of the Lord—an attitude which contributed to even greater hostility toward him on the part of the extreme Orthodox.

The legacy of Rabbi Kuk has not dwindled, nor has its vitality diminished as it illumines the path of many a Jew in Israel today who reflects his role as a member of his people, a citizen of the world and an individual in his own right.

In summary, Kuk's fertile mind, radiant personality and illustrious career present the following lasting contributions: (a) In *religion* he attempted to adapt a two thousand year tradition of a people in exile to the new realities of a nation on its own soil. (The process has not yet run its course.) In the integration of religious heritage and modern life, it called for a remolding of the latter and a re-interpretation of the former. It is largely Kuk's achievement that, in their current setting in Israel, religious authority and free speculation can flourish in more or less peaceful coexistence in a society where there is no marked separation between Church and State.

(b) His *nationalism*, embedded in the religious situation, is transcending in its universal ramifications and spiritual overtones, spelling out human love and understanding beyond the borders of state and nation.

(c) His impact went beyond intellectual formulation. His philosophy forged a base for creative and satisfying *experience*. From Kuk's mystic piety there emanated a *joie de vivre*, nourished by a deep faith that makes for the individual's dynamic and joyous involvement in the process of national reconstruction. The new life in Palestine became a link in the chain of historic community—in Kuk's own formulation,—as "the old is renovated and the new is sanctified." In essence, it provided an antidote for an abrasive secularism, surpassing the latter in its humanistic and humanitarian thrust. It established the human condition for harmonious involvement, meaningful expression and spiritual development of men and women joined together by inspired endeavor to realize Divine promise and human fulfillment.

The Zionist Debate—

A SUMMING UP

I

Nineteenth century events in Jewish life paralleled at an accelerated pace four centuries of European developments. The modern age in Western civilization is marked by: religious reformation, scientific discoveries, geographic expansion, economic reorganization, the rise of secular literature and the awakening of national consciousness. Similarly, but in a quarter of the time which it took Europe to pass from comparative medieval darkness to the illumination of modernity, European Jewry, representing quantitatively and qualitatively the major segment of a world-wide people, rushed through the same stages. Religious reform in Germany was followed by: scholarly research in Jewish history, religion and institutions; mass emigration from Eastern Europe leading to the emergence of new Jewish communities in North and South America, South Africa, Australia and Palestine; economic transformation from shiftless ghetto economy to advanced commerce and labor; growth of a modern Hebrew and Yiddish literature, press, theatre and music; and a dynamic nationalism directed toward reconstitution of scattered Jewry on its ancient soil.

The last stage, which culminated in the establishment of the State of Israel in 1948, initially brought forth fructifying theoretical speculations, many of which crystallized into party platforms and institutional programs, supplying the ideological foundations for the social and cultural values of existing Israel society and the official as well as inherent goals of education. The major contributions have been analyzed in the preceding chapters which contain the essential and influential ideas of twelve political, literary and scholarly personalities, selected from the galaxy of Zionist luminaries. These were the leading intellectual pioneers, essentially the founding fathers of modern Israel. They brought forth the ideas and served as the architects, while the function and privilege of becoming the builders was left to the statesmen and leaders who succeeded them. Weizmann, Ben Gurion, Ben Zvi and Jabotinsky were the men of fate and action who forged the Zionist movement and fashioned the State of Israel. The faith, inspiration and blueprints were supplied by the men of vision who had preceded them.

The Jewish problem, as it was seen by Jewish intellectuals in the sixty year period after 1865, (roughly between the American Civil War and the Russian Revolution) was viewed in political, economic, psychological, cultural and religious perspectives. Many intellectuals sought a solution, but relatively few left the imprint of their ideas on the course of Jewish history. And, as in the classic case of the elephant, each touched a different part of the body under investigation. In retrospect, none was wrong and yet none was completely right. A subsequent generation of disciples and practical men gathered the diversified elements into an all-inclusive pattern. Or was it the natural interaction of the processes of life that formed the synthesis?

In seeking a solution to the Jewish problem, the fertile minds involved were influenced by their own *milieux,* under the impact of which they acquired insights into contemporaneous conditions, offered appraisals of historic phenomena and arrived at formulae for a projected future. Though they pointed in the same direction, they were propelled by different backgrounds, motives and convictions. Jewish intellectuals and professionals of Western and Central Europe, moved by the new spirit of national self-determination and unification around them, and embattled in the struggle for civil liberties for Jews, were foremost in advocating an autonomous state to take its place among the nations of the world. East European thinkers and writers, steeped in the indigenous rich culture of compact Jewish masses, and fearful of the sweeping tide of assimilation inundating the ghetto walls of age-old Jewish spiritual isolation, were turning to Zion restored for possible reinforcement as well as redirection to bolster the declining strength of the ranks of the faithful. Searching souls, caught in the waves of mass emigration, detached from the moorings of ancient traditions, while purposelessly adrift in the turbulent waters of various 'isms,' were seeking an anchor for their troubled spirits. Deeply pious personalities, ablaze with the flame of religious fervor, gravitated to the Holy Land and the wells of inspiration. Lost souls, returning home, sought renewed meaning in ancient aspirations. Palestine was their common focus, a beacon of light; and it was as if each individual saw it in a different color of the spectrum as it appeared within his line of vision.

The spiritual pioneers who planted the seeds, the produce of which is still harvested in Israel, were as diversified in their backgrounds as they were in their thinking. They came from different countries, were publicly involved in several others, they wrote in different languages and expressed themselves through different genres. Geographically, two (Hess and Herzl) were born and raised in Central Europe, while the others came from areas under Russian domination, such as Latvia, Lithuania, Poland, the Ukraine and Russia itself. Linguistically, seven of them expounded their Zionist theories in Hebrew, some of them in German (Hess, Herzl and Pinsker) others in Yiddish (Syrkin and Borochov) and one in Russian (Borochov). As to their literary classifications, three were novelists, (Smolenskin, Berdichevsky and Brenner); one was a theologian (Kuk); and the others were journalists and social analysts. Their creative writing took place in Palestine (four) Russia (three), Austria (two), Germany (one), France (one) and America (one). Three lived for some time in the United States (Ben Yehuda, Syrkin and Borochov), and five never saw Palestine.

What they all shared was a profound preoccupation with the problems of the Jewish people, crystallizing in the conviction that the minority status was at the root of all evil, and that Israel offers the ultimate, if not the total solution. Much of what they said and wrote has not withstood the test of time; yet a good deal of their fertile thought blossomed forth with a fragrance that has not evaporated from the atmosphere of Israel today. The preceding pages attempt to record briefly these contributions in value categories operative in Israel society and related to its educational philosophy.

II

To grasp the Jewish problem in its intricacy and entirety, one must divest himself of American concepts and enter into the social and intellectual European climate of pre-World War I. Homogeneous ethnic groups with common geographic, historic, linguistic and—with few exceptions—religious ties, comprised the majority populations of various nations. In this setting nineteenth century liberalism held out the promise of freedom for the individual. Extension of democratic privileges to the individual was considered in these circles to be highly commendable, provided that the individual was integrated within the national religio-cultural framework. Enjoyment of similar rights by a minority group *per se,* was inconceivable. Thus, religious and ethnic-cultural pluralism in the American democratic sense was, to say the least, unappreciated. Cultural, and to a degree religious abdication was the price the minority paid for the majority acceptance of its individual members. Characteristic of this attitude was the statement of one of the leaders of the French Revolution, pleading for equal rights for Jews: "To Jews as a nation—nothing; but to Jews as human beings—everything."[238]

The Zionist formula in its various versions sought to respond to the total challenge confronting the Jewish people and the Jewish individual in the three areas of physical and material security, religious and cultural expression and psychological needs. Each of the three areas of concern and the different Zionist responses are traced briefly in the following:

(a) A century after the French Revolution broke the shackles of medieval relegation of the Jews to an inferior civil status, the Jewish problem was no less severe than before. The physical threat prevailed. Anti-Semitism was as rampant in advanced Western Europe as it was in the retarded Russian Empire. Jewish separatism in the latter and increasing assimilation in the former, generated prejudice and animosity. Nothing short of total dissolution of Jews as a group could eliminate bias and its concomitant effects.

Whence this anti-Semitism?

Hess analyzed it as an instinctive embedded race hatred accentuated by religious and cultural factors. He regarded this biologically rooted racial bigotry as characteristic of some nations, particularly Germany (an observation corroborated in the tragic events of the World War II era.)

Pinsker diagnosed it primarily as a psychosis, "Judeophobia", though often with political and economic ramifications. It is a Platonic hatred aroused by the abnormal condition of the Jews as a walking national skeleton among living people who react with fear and suspicion. The general distrust of the alien, aggravated by the unnatural circumstances of Israel's survival in the midst of nations, becomes an irrational—almost irresistible—force in the minds of the Gentiles.

Hess's anthropologic-psychological explanation of anti-Semitism, and Pinsker's socio-psychological analysis, are followed by Herzl's political conclusions. Herzl perceives it as something deeper than religious intolerance or social prejudice (as Smolenskin previously believed) that can be eliminated or at least mitigated by education. It is a national problem requiring a political solution to be offered by an aroused world opinion.

Syrkin is cognizant of the historic clash of values between Jew and Gentile, greatly intensified by the stratification of national social entities feeding the fires of hostility toward Jews. And Borochov recognizes that in the course of the economic history of every society the enterprising spirit of the Jewish entrepreneur runs the gamut from favorable acceptance to hostile competition in the field of labor. In the final stage of economic development, the Jewish proletariat is inevitably removed from an effective role in the class struggle antecedent to the new social order.

A Jewish state is, therefore, the answer for those Jews unable or unwilling to remain victimized by the scourge of anti-Semitism, regardless of its origin. Furthermore, the creation and existence of a viable state for the Jewish people removes the stigma of homelessness (Pinsker) and national inferiority status (Ben Yehuda), and serves as a haven of refuge (Herzl) and economic safety valve (Syrkin), or a strategic base for the class struggle (Borochov) in alleviating the pressures—psychological, social, political and economic—upon those Jews who remain in their adopted homelands.

(b) Simultaneous with the response to the threat of anti-Semitism, thinking Jews were formulating an answer to the challenge of assimilation. The Jewish problem was defined by other men of thought in cultural rather than physical terms. To them it was essentially a question of how to retain Jewish distinctiveness in its authentic and creative forms, amidst engulfing conformity. It was more the revival of Judaism than the survival of Jews that preoccupied them. Acclimated to the political and economic disadvantages of Jewish life in Eastern Europe, and consciously moved by an abiding faith in nineteenth century liberalism, they beheld with apprehension the crumbling walls of an age-old pattern of living, exposing the rising generation to the beckoning breezes of alien cultures.

Smolenskin at first conceived of a "spiritual nationalism" differing in kind from ethnic nationalism, the former to be expressed in spiritual values (which he did not enumerate) and acting as a cohesive and protective factor for Jewish survival. Literary Hebrew was to be the medium as well as the substance of the message, and this was also accepted by Ahad Ha'am who identified the permanent values in Jewish historical experience and re-defined them in contemporary terms while projecting their revitalization in a "spiritual centre" in Palestine. The latter was to exert a centrifugal force revitalizing and unifying scattered Jewry throughout the world. Ben Yehuda, whose concept of nationalism was unabashedly removed from spiritual considerations, established in theory and practice the condition of a living Hebrew tongue as a major force in Jewish unity, providing the linguistic form for the cultural content fostered by others. Kuk restored to cultural nationalism and its secularized spirituality the traditional religious frame, charging it with the ineffable, though nonetheless real power for individual, national and universal salvation. Ahad Ha'am concluded that a two thousand year old religious civilization had ceased to function effectively as the cohesive force in Jewish survival and, therefore, should be remodeled in intellectually more acceptable forms, emanating from a spiritual power-base in Palestine. Kuk, without objecting to the diagnosis, prescribed the conventional formula recharged and redirected with increasing potency in the blending with modern nationalism. He converted Ahad Ha'am's sociology into Jewish mysticism and invested the reconstituted center with salutary powers efficacious beyond its borders. The effect would be to support the retreating tradition against the onslaught of assimilation.

The common denominator in the secular and religious formulations is one of spiritual rebirth. A Jewish society in Palestine, flourishing without restriction in a free and hospitable climate, will take root and produce a living culture of institutions and values, linked to the past and operative in the present. The rejuvenated culture will be spiritual-ethical in character, intellectual in content,

Hebrew in form, national in scope and universal in focus.

(c) The political and cultural aims of Zionism directed towards the physical and spiritual survival of Jews and Judaism respectively, were complemented by psychological motives concerned with the wholesomeness of the individual Jewish personality. Keen observers of Jewish life in European "exile" were conscious of the emotional pressures, mental aberrations and social maladjustment of the individual Jew brought about by the conditions—some of his own making—under which he lived. Zionism made the diagnosis and offered the therapy for the disturbed Jewish personality.

Berdichevsky put the blame on a dust-gathering bookish heritage, overladen with pietistic and moralizing cargo. Opening the windows to Europe, casting off the antiquated yoke of ages, reducing the ethical overemphasis, responding to the aesthetic in art and life, substituting brawn for brain—these were the actual rejections and affirmations of Berdichevsky as he envisaged a "normal" Jewish personality, once again restored to its human form, as it originally flourished in ancient times on its own soil.

Brenner groped more deeply into the inner conflicts of the Jewish soul. He contemplated the frustrations of existence as a member of a despised group. He took account of the psychological toll resulting from rejection and humiliation by an alien world. He protested against the intellectual sophistry, the moral distortion, the social maladjustment, the emotional confusion, the economic unproductivity and uprootedness—all of which added up to a sick, delinquent Jewish personality reduced to subhuman dimensions. And a Jewish society in Palestine was the one last hope for a modicum of recovery.

A. D. Gordon prescribed the formula for the soothing balm to relieve the aches of pseudo-life in the Diaspora and its restoration to fullness in Palestine. A life of labor in the bosom of nature would open well-springs of psychological strength, providing the required therapy for the disturbed Jewish soul. The healthful effects of harmony, security and fulfillment, with the accruing benefits of character-building, soul-enriching and emotionally gratifying experiences would redeem the individual from the creeping dehumanization which paralyzed his very being.

III

The *individual* motif in Zionism, incisively introspective in focus and pragmatically oriented in formula, blended with the *political* program and *cultural* theme in the all-embracing challenge of Jewish redemption. Palestine was to become the social laboratory for renewed and emerging values operative in the social, economic and psychological realms. Nothing short of complete metamorphosis was the hope of the founder of political Zionism. "A new face, thank God, to the Jewish community. Only then will Zion be Zion."[239]

Characteristic of this faith are the words of the most revered leader of the Israel labor movement, Berl Katznelson. He stated that:

> Zionism offered a totally new scope beyond the borders of village, province and country. . . . It discovered and developed the Land-of-Israel man whose deliberations and powers were directed toward change in the general situation. . . . It brought forth in the open the Jewish personality embracing nation and world.[240]

That this was not mere lip service nor exuberant verbosity is demonstrated by the testimony of the renowned non-Jewish historian who has never been accused of sympathy for Zionism—Arnold J. Toynbee:

> . . . they set out defiantly and enthusiastically to turn themselves into manual laborers instead of city dwellers, into producers instead of middlemen, into agriculturalists instead of financiers, into warriors instead of shopkeepers.[241]

The following is an attempt to identify these pivotal values crystallized in the modern Israel *milieu* as they relate to vital issues in Jewish life, tracing their origin to the authoritative dreamers and thinkers presented in the preceding chapters.

(a) In the hierarchy of social attitudes and values as they apply to the pursuit of livelihood, *physical labor* occupies an exalted position. The Marxist, Borochov, accepted it as economic necessity but was compelled to place a higher premium on heavy industry because of its potential key role in the class struggle. Gordon exalted glorified labor, elevating it to a religion. He affirmed that in the life of labor, the innate spiritual powers of man are released as he relates himself to the cosmos, society and self. Brenner perceived in physical work both a preventative and an elixir for the ills of mind and psyche of the modern Jew.

Lifting physical work from its humble footstool to the seat of glory was a philosophical proposition bolstered by political and economic necessity, making for balanced occupational differentiation in Israel economy. Menial work and its technical and specialized operations frequently enjoyed status above "white collar" and commercial employment in inverse ratio to the scale of merit in vogue for ages. That this was nourished by the pioneer spirit of idealism, needs no elaboration. It has been consciously cultivated by the highest echelon, as demonstrated by Premier Ben Gurion's literal return to the plow after retirement from office in 1953 and again in 1963.

(b) In advocating the importance of "productive"

labor, Zionism set a premium on *agriculture* as most desirable. Brenner and Gordon rhapsodized over rural life and farming as a livelihood. Urbanization was considered largely at fault for many of the problems of the Jews, spiritual and economic, social and psychological. Reconstitution of a segment of Jewry in Palestine into an agricultural society was a political necessity, an economic requirement and a spiritual indispensability. Decades of such orientation have effected a situation where youth of the highest moral and intellectual caliber has turned to pioneer farming in the fulfillment of aspirations toward service and career. Though only about 15% of Israel's population in 1970 is found in the agricultural sector, there is an organized movement from the city to the farm, particularly among young people. This is no less motivated by ideology than by the military considerations requiring the establishment of frontier settlements.

(c) Proletarianization and agrarianization of merchants and professionals are inseparable from *social idealism and experimentation*. These are not limited control situations but are of national ramifications. Hess had related the rebirth of the Jewish nation to the revolutionary movement of the age, envisaging a society built on socialist foundations with special emphasis on land nationalization. The latter was gradually realized through the Jewish National Fund which was organized in 1901 as the land purchasing agency of the Zionist movement to acquire land as the inalienable property of the Jewish people. It has been financed chiefly by mass subscriptions throughout the world. It continues to hold title to expanding cultivated, industrialized and settled areas in Israel.

Herzl contemplated a seven-hour workday as exemplifying social progress. Ahad Ha'am made social justice the cornerstone of his philosophical edifice. Syrkin closed the gap between Zionism and socialism, hoping for a new socialist society in Palestine. Borochov projected a communist economic system. Gordon identified himself with the *kibbutz* movement consisting mostly of rural settlements operating as local units on the communistic principle of collective ownership of property and consumer goods, combined with bold social experimentation in group living. Brenner is still regarded as founder of the *Histadrut,* the general labor federation of Israel. And Rabbi Kuk surprised the Orthodox camp by offering religious sanction for workers' strikes.

What the diverse programs share is a determination to build a new society free from the chronic ills of European economy. They all aim toward economic reorganization without exploitation of labor. The formulators of these various programs draw from the ethical teachings of the Prophets, the social ideals of the Jewish code of law, idealistic liberalism and contemporary socialism.

Within this ideological context, and as a result of local historical conditions (including the fact that in Israel, labor and national collective enterprise preceded private capital), Israel is to an impressive extent a planned economy, controlled by organized labor with a collectivist sector largely in agriculture. Social consciousness is very keen, the labor movement in particular being imbued with a sense of mission beyond its trade union interests. Within this frame of reference social idealism, in economic terms, is more than altruistic behavior for the elite; it is a national trait cultivated and superimposed—with both the positive and negative connotations of the latter term—on the developing economy of an emerging society.

(d) Israel, which came into being through the combined efforts of *Jews in Palestine and abroad,* is inexorably bound to the far-flung Jewish settlements throughout the world. This is regarded as a circumstance of fate as well as an article of faith. On the one hand, Israel looks beyond for continued support of the nascent State, its welfare depending on a favorable political climate, increased economic aid and investment, and augmented, untapped sources of immigration. In exchange, as Ahad Ha'am envisaged, Israel offers cultural values to cement the unity and retain the integrity of the other eleven million members of the Jewish people dispersed over the globe. While Ahad Ha'am was concerned with Israel-inspired *content* of historical continuity and contemporary validity in binding Jews together, Ben Yehuda looked to the *form* of a revived Hebrew tongue for the bond among scattered members of one people. To him, the Hebrew medium was the message itself. In the consensus that prevailed, Jewish life of the future was to appear as a wheel, with Israel as the hub and the Diaspora as the encircling rim, held together by spiritual spokes. The functions may not have been equal, with the periphery more subject to outer pressure and dents than the center; but the unity of the whole had to be maintained for the wheel to remain in motion.

In such a conception, the Israeli recognizes the partnership—though junior partnership—of the Diaspora Jew in the national revival. The abundant benefits flourishing in the reassembled Jewish nation on its own soil are to be shared to a lesser yet significant degree by Jews everywhere. This refers to values and privileges which are universal and ethical (Hess and Ahad Ha'am), national and linguistic (Ben Yehuda), psychological (Brenner), introspectively spiritual (Gordon), religious (Kuk), and aesthetic (Berdichevsky). Herzl envisaged political legal advantages, and Pinsker projected an improved social image for Jews residing outside of Palestine after the state was established.

Ahad Ha'am's affirmation of extra-territorial Judaism, as a challenge and a comparatively lesser but still undeniable opportunity, is offset by a negation of Diaspora Judaism on the part of other Zionist spokesmen. Herzl had conceded, without protest, the deliberate disengagement from Jewish identification by elements choosing to remain permanently outside of the rebuilt homeland. The traditional definition of the state of Diaspora as divine punishment for national misconduct in ancient days is reinterpreted by Brenner as sinful existence *per se,* falling short of human dimensions. Others, viewing life in the Diaspora from different points of view, found it inadequate and inferior when measured by the realistic and aesthetic standards and requirements of modern civilization (Berdichevsky), without the opportunity for personal fulfillment (Gordon), with an unbalanced and unproductive economy in inevitably deteriorating conditions (Syrkin and Borochov), politically unprotected (Herzl), socially humiliated (Pinsker), and spiritually impoverished (Kuk). In the light of contrasting conditions, the Israeli can look at Diaspora Jewry either with myopic vision as satellites reflecting the new light shining forth from Zion, or with the jaundiced eye of upbraiding criticism and invidious comparison.

The two views of Exile—shackles of captivity or rearguard of advancing columns—create not an ambivalence but a dichotomy of attitude toward the non-Israeli Jew. Alternately, these reactions harmonize in strengthening the inner security of the Israelis as they face the uncertainties and exigencies of unrelenting military and economic threats by hostile neighbors.

(e) The modern Jew has had to re-examine his *attitude toward the Gentile.* With the transfer from a minority state of weakness to a majority status of power, the normalization of Jewish life required a clarification of relationship to the world at large. What is involved as a result of such deliberations are not only attitudes reflected in policies toward others; it also invites frequent re-evaluation of oneself.

The selection of Israel is a theological concept which, deprived of its supernatural overtones, permeates the secularized circles of modern Israel as well. Ancient Israel was chosen by God to be "a light of the nations."[242] Israel today is to fulfill its destiny by exemplified leadership of a new society founded on and guided by the highest norms of social justice. Jewish nationalism was to embrace mankind in its ethical message and social experimentation. Hess prophesied the spiritual possibilities of Jewish revival, claiming a nationalism confluent with universalism and humanitarianism. Herzl harbored aspirations of social legislation, which though more modest, were advanced even for our day. Ahad Ha'am dreamt of the "spirit of Judaism" creating a utopian, or at least exemplary society, erecting "a cultural center in Zion as a great service to humanity at large."[243] Syrkin aspired toward socialism that shall come forth out of Zion. Gordon entertained the vision of the New Man. And Kuk saw him sanctified in the prophetic role of serving mankind.

To Herzl, Israel may have been a haven of refuge from European persecution, but it was no escape from European civilization. To avoid the economic and social maladies of European capitalism was one thing; to reject Western culture was something else. Israel, geographically in Asia, was to remain spiritually in Western Europe, adapting what is best in Western civilization to its own needs. Ahad Ha'ạm objected to Europe's invasion of Jewry's spiritual domain. He recommended emulation instead of assimilation as a creative cultural process frought with great promise. Israel society was to be modern in form but Jewish in character, taking its place among the societies of man. This was the conservative approach of an authoritative spokesman for the Jewish revolution.

The radical sector, led by Berdichevsky, took sharp issue with this position. If two thousand years of Jewish life had been a tragic error—as he insisted—then nothing short of surgery would accomplish the transformation. Jewish society was to be Western in character, modern in form, secular in spirit, Jewish in constitution. As against Ahad Ha'am's Jewish ethics, he raised the banner of Greek aesthetics. Art, music, and drama, unencumbered by historical baggage, would flourish in the Hebrew vernacular. The Jews would be a nation like all nations.

Time has healed the breach between the ideologies in conflict. A sense of mission inspires men and women engaged in establishing a society founded on social idealism, supported by historical values and elevated by cultural interests. Simultaneously, a desire for normalization of life in the free development of a culture liberated from the chains or the challenges of obligation, characterizes the evolving pattern of Israel values and institutions. Perhaps the Israeli desires neither to resent the Gentile nor adulate him; he wants only to live in a world big enough for both of them.

(f) The role of *religion* in Israel is a controversial issue, unattenuated even while other problems are reduced in intensity, as a people deepens its stakes in a new land. The relationship of Synagogue and State is a subject of debate in government, society and education. For the first time in millenia, Judaism is the religion of the governing majority, faced with the opportunity and the difficulty of translating what has been largely an academic code of law into practical reality. An ambitious, all-inclusive jurisprudence embracing ritual, economic and social behaviour—virtually all of life—attempted by the Jewish code of law, is unprepared for the exigencies and contingencies of a self-governing society disposed to secularization.

Zionism has been a link in historical continuity as well as a break with tradition. Nourished by the spiritual heritage of national romanticism, historical messianism, and ethical consciousness, the Zionist movement nevertheless represented a revolt against religious authority and existing patterns of institutions and values. In rebelling against the passive resistance to the pressures of the Diaspora, it espoused norms deviating from religiously sanctioned standards. This was initially sensed by the majority of the Orthodox community and accounted for its adamant opposition to it.

Freedom, or the quest for freedom in its individual as well as national forms, is an expanding process diffused from the political and economic to the religious. This is true not only of "pagan" Berdichevsky and critical Brenner, but holds as well for the spiritual-center-minded Ahad Ha'am. The latter, in his espousal of the ethics of Jewish religion and history, never accepted the binding ritual of Judaism with its discipline regulating the individual, family and group, in all their diversified relations of living. Already the mystic Hess hinted at religious revisions necessary to a revitalization of Judaism when Jewry returns to its homeland. The leading Orthodox spokesman for Zionism, Chief Rabbi Kuk, was alone among religious authorities to attempt even cautiously the adaptation of religious law to the contemporary needs in Palestine. The founding fathers of the State of Israel expediently retained the *status quo* inherited from the British regime, in the government-recognized and autonomous Jewish religious courts (also Mohammedan and Christian), with authority to legislate marriage, divorce, Sabbath laws and related matters. Religious political parties (four in number, recently reduced to three) jealously guard this system and aim for its expansion. Articulate secular forces are aided by the unfavorable reaction to the combination of politics and religion, in advocating complete separation of Synagogue and State. The historic synonymity of Jews as a people with Judaism as a religion makes such severance problematic if not enigmatic, pointing out once again the difficulty of applying an American standard (separation of Church and State) to Israel realities.*

This dichotomy of authoritarian religion and rampant secularism is, in the final analysis, indicative of a society in formation, as a cultural lag follows technological and social acceleration. The conflict between religion and secularism gives way to processes of co-existence ultimately leading to a synthesis. These pangs of growth are bound to cease if Israel is to fulfill its destiny. Already searching souls among its intellectuals and educators are groping for a more spiritual orientation and religious content. The public school curriculum beginning with the 1957-8 academic year has been enriched with a "Jewish consciousness" program of instruction in ritual and religious institutions. That this innovation is more in keeping with Smolenskin's and Ahad Ha'am's positive affirmation of tradition than with the iconoclastic tendencies of Berdichevsky, Brenner and Ben Yehuda, is quite obvious. In time, overtures from the religious camp may eliminate the

* Jewish communities outside of Israel are not beset by the same problem since their minority status makes the bulk of religious jurisprudence legally inoperative and compels religious identification as the only form of Jewish expression. Secular Jewishness, as an official form of identification which once flourished in Eastern Europe and to a degree in America, is virtually disappearing from the Western democracies.

tension and pave the way for a genuine religious revival. The sensational events of the Six Day War in June, 1967, mainly the dramatic encounters with the Jewish Holy Places, hitherto out of reach, appeared to have aroused intense religious feelings among the secular as well. Though this may be a momentary experience without lasting merit, the war did cement Jewish unity with an intensity unprecedented throughout three thousand years of Jewish history, and paved the road to mutual understanding among adversaries, the militantly religious and brazenly secular not excluded.

(g) The ethnic penchant for matters of the *mind* has been preserved in Israel, though not without considerable redirection. The Zionist preoccupation with productivization of Jewish masses in industry (Borochov) and agriculture (Gordon) was directed more against commercial and clerical occupations than against intellectual pursuits. Herzl, however, felt that there was an over-abundance of "intellectual mediocrities" within the Jewish group. Personages such as Brenner, exerting a powerful influence on the pioneer sector in Palestine, were derisively hostile to Jewish intelligentsia in its over-intellectualism with the concomitant economic uprootedness and psychological maladjustment. Berdichevsky envisaged the robust farmer and laborer leading a healthy, satisfying life unaffected by intellectual and moral sophistication.

Yet the Jewish intellectual qualities and cultural commitments have been nourished and made to flourish within the pattern of Israel life. If the English-speaking world created the gentleman-farmer prototype, Israel evolved the student-farmer who combines tilling of the soil with the study of the book. He is imbued with a sense of mission, serving in the vanguard of a people on the march. Ahad Ha'am's disciple, Chaim Weizmann, (subsequently the first president of Israel) was instrumental in establishing the Hebrew University in Jerusalem (1925) dedicated to the furtherance of Jewish scholarship, liberal arts and the sciences. This was undertaken at a time when such a project was deemed a premature luxury.

Israel socio-philosophical and educational norms blend the intellectual tradition of historical Judaism with the practical, physical and technological needs of a rehabilitated Jewry. They bring together the moral values of the past along with the aesthetic and practical interests of the present. The extremist splinter groups of the religious authoritarian *Neturai Karta* and the isolationist libertarian *Canaanites* may jealously guard their own uncompromising platforms. However, what is generally accepted and formally advocated, reflected in official pronouncement, creative literature and organized education, suggests a balance between mind and body, the intellectual and the practical, the moral and the aesthetic. Comparatively new to the conventional Jewish scene are phenomena such as physical culture, competitive sports, extensive agricultural, scientific and mechanical training and art schools. These are essentially, though not exclusively, products of the Zionist revolution plotted by the inspired visionaries in the galaxy of personages who light up the horizon of Israel to the present day. Their paths, joined together in the dream which became the reality of modern Israel, have been traced in this book.

Notes

1. Cf. Leopold Laufer, *Israel and the Developing Countries* (New York: The Twentieth Century Fund, 1967).

2. For a full and absorbing report read Shlomo Barer, *The Magic Carpet* (New York: Harper, 1952).

3. *Israel 1954* (New York: Israel Office of Information, 1955), p. 219.

4. For a comprehensive view of the *kibbutz* see Ester Tauber, *Molding Society to Man* (New York: Bloch Publishing Co., 1955).

5. "The Talmud Student," *Selected Poems of Hayyim Nahman Bialik* translated from the Hebrew (N.Y.: Bloch Publishing Co. 1965) p. 29.

6. Simon Halkin, *Modern Hebrew Literature: Trends and Values* (New York: Schocken Books, 1950), p. 104.

7. *Ibid.,* p. 101.

8. Cf. Shalom Spiegel, *Hebrew Reborn* (New York: Macmillan, 1930).

9. Joseph Dunner, *The Republic of Israel: Its History and its Promise* (New York: McGraw-Hill Book Co., 1950), pp. 93-94.

10. A peeved Martin Luther turned to diatribe against Jews when they refused to accept his "liberalized" version of Christianity.

11. Cf. Joseph Klausner, *History of Modern Hebrew Literature,* vol. I, in Hebrew (Jerusalem: Hebrew University Press, 1948).

12. Rufus Learsi, *Fulfillment: The Epic Story of Zionism* (Cleveland: World Publishing Co., 1951), citing Noah p. 32.

13. Hazan and Feller, *The History of Zionism,* in Hebrew (Jerusalem: Kiryat Sefer, 1948), pp. 31-38.

14. Translated by Maurice Samuel, *Harvest in the Desert* (Philadelphia: Jewish Publication Society, 1944), p. 50.

15. See Jacob de Haas, Introduction to *A Jewish State* by Theodor Herzl (New York: The Maccabaean Pub. Co., 1904) p. x.

16. Yitzchak Greenbaum, *The Zionist Movement, in* Hebrew (Jerusalem: Mass, 1942), Book II, p. 8.

17. Simon Halkin, *Modern Hebrew Literature . . . op. cit.,* citing the Vitkin Manifesto, pp. 90-97.

18. Cf. Joseph Baratz, *A Village by the Jordan: the Story of Degania* (New York: Roy Publishers, 1955).

19. Cf. Melford E. Spiro, *Kibbutz: Venture in Utopia* (Cambridge: Harvard University Press, 1956). Murray Weingarten, *Life on a Kibbutz* (New York: Reconstructionist Press, 1955).

20. *Book of Documents,* Submitted to the General Assembly of the United Nations (New York: Jewish Agency for Palestine, 1948).

21. Cf. Moshe Pearlman, *The Army of Israel* (New York: Philosophical Library, 1950).

22. Irving Miller, *The Zionist Movement Today (*New York: 1950), pp. 26, 30, 35.

23. *Rome and Jerusalem,* trans. Meyer Waxman (New York: Bloch Publishing Co., 1945), p. 40.

24. Sydney Hook, "Karl Marx and Moses Hess," *The New International,* I (December, 1934), p. 140.

25. *Economic-Philosophical Manuscripts,* written in 1844 but first published posthumously in German in 1932. In English, International Publishers: 1964.

26. Moses Hess, *Rome and Jerusalem, op. cit.,* p. 60.

27. *Ibid.,* p. 62.

28. *Ibid.,* p. 40.
29. *Ibid.,* p. 106.
30. *Ibid.,* p. 111.
31. *Ibid.,* p. 139.
32. *Ibid.,* p. 157, 158.
33. *Ibid.,* p. 146.
34. Moses Hess, *Selected Writings,* trans. Jeshurun Keshet, in Hebrew (Jerusalem: The Zionist Library, 1954), p. 182.
35. *Ibid.,* p. 129.
36. Solomon Grayzel, *The History of the Jews* (Philadelphia: Jewish Publication Society, 1953), pp. 573-594.
37. Moses Hess, *Rome and Jerusalem, op. cit.,* p. 96.
38. *Ibid.,* p. 35.
39. *Ibid.,* p. 144.
40. *Ibid.,* p. 158.
41. *Ibid.,* p. 197.
42. Simon Dubnow, *World History of the Jewish People,* in Yiddish (Buenos Aires; Confederacion procultura Judia, 1955), vol. IX, p. 277.
43. A two volume edition of his selected works edited by Martin Buber appeared in Hebrew translation (Jerusalem: World Zionist Organization, 1954).
44. Yitzchak Greenbaum, *The Zionist Movement, op. cit.,* p. 32.
45. Hazan and Feller, *History of Zionism, op. cit.,* p. 46.
46. Peretz Smolenskin, "A Time to Plant," *Pangs of a Nation* (anthology), vol. I, in Hebrew, J. Ovsi *et. al.* (New York: Israel Matz Fund, 1938), pp. 53, 55, 56.
47. Peretz Smolenskin, "The Jewish Problem—a Life Problem," *ibid.,* p. 60.
48. *Ibid.,* p. 64.
49. Yehezkel Kaufmann, *Exile and Estrangement,* in Hebrew (Tel Aviv: Dvir, 1930), vol. II, p. 289.
50. Peretz Smolenskin, "Let us Seek our Way," *The Book of Zionism: Hibat Zion Era,* Vol. II book I. ed. sh. Yavnieli, in Hebrew (Tel Aviv: Dvir 1944) p. 122
51. *Ibid.,* p. 141.

52. His leading and voluminous novels are still unavailable in English translation.

53. Joseph Klausner, *The Foundation Builders of the State of Israel,* in Hebrew (Jerusalem: Achiasaf, 1953), p. 28.

54. *The Book of Zionism: Hibat Zion Era.* vol. II Book II. *op. cit.,* p. 12.

55. *Ibid.,* p. 13.

56. Joseph Klausner, *Foundation Builders of the State of Israel, op. cit.,* p. 61.

57. Rufus Learsi, *Fulfillment: The Epic Story of Zionism, op. cit.,* p. 44.

58. Leo Pinsker, *Auto-Emancipation,* trans. C. S. Blondheim (New York: Zionist Organization of America, 1948) p. 4.

59. *Ibid.,* p. 6.

60. *Ibid.,* p. 12.

61. *Ibid.*

62. *Ibid.,* p. 27.

63. *Ibid.,* p. 31.

64. *Ibid.,* p. 34.

65. *Ibid.,* p. 35.

66. Eliezer Ben Yehuda, *Collected Works,* vol. I, in Hebrew (Jerusalem: Hozaa La' or Lezecher Eliezer Ben-Yehuda, 1941) pp. 6, 8.

67. *Ibid.,* p. 7.

68. *Ibid.,* p. 31.

69. *Ibid.,* p. 29.

70. Eliezer Ben Yehuda, "Judaism and its Future," *Selected Hebrew Essays,* ed. Becker and Schpan, in Hebrew (Tel Aviv: Gazit, 1953) p. 147.

71. Eliezer Ben Yehuda, *Collected Works, op. cit.,* p. 77.

72. Robert St. John, *Tongue of the Prophets* (Garden City: Doubleday and Co., 1952).

73. U. Tulkiss, "Eliezer Ben Yehuda: Thirty Years After His Death," *Metzudah,* vol. VII, ed. S. Rawidowicz, in Hebrew (London: Ararat Publication Society, 1954), p. 624.

74. A. Orinovsky, *History of Modern Hebrew Literature,* vol. II, in Hebrew (Tel Aviv: 1950) p. 61.

75. U. Tulkiss, *op. cit.,* p. 629.
76. Robert St. John, *op. cit.,* p. 367.
77. Ludwig Lewisohn, ed. *Theodor Herzl: A Protrait for This Age* (Cleveland: World Publishing Co., 1955) p. 52.
78. Theodor Herzl, *The Jewish State.* (New York: American Zionist Emergency Council, 1946) Alex Bein, biographer, citing Herzl, p. 34.
79. *Ibid.*
80. *Ibid.,* p. 92.
81. *Ibid.,* p. 74.
82. The analysis is noteworthy as a prognosis of the Nazi mania of later years, and its catastrophic effects.
83. *Ibid.,* p. 94. This function was finally granted the Zionist Organization after the first World War.
84. *Ibid.,* p. 119. In the initial stage of activities the latter necessarily became the chief source—a manifestation of faith and support by the people.
85. *Ibid.,* p. 82.
86. *Ibid.,* p. 155.
87. Arthur Koestler has advocated the same idea and has aroused considerable opposition to his views.
88. Theodor Herzl, *Old-New Land.* Trans. L. Levensohn (New York: Bloch Publishing Co., 1941) p. 178.
89. Theodor Herzl, *The Jewish State, op. cit.,* p. 156.
90. *Ibid.,* p. 156-157.
91. Theodor Herzl, *Old-New Land, op. cit.,* translator's introduction, p. xi.
92. *Ibid.,* p. 82.
93. Ludwig Lewisohn, *op. cit.,* p. 57.
94. Chaim Weizmann, *op. cit.,* p. 43.
95. Ludwig Lewisohn, *op. cit.,* p. 61.
96. Theodor Herzl, *The Jewish State, op. cit.,* p. 72.
97. *Vision of Herzl: Selections,* in Hebrew(Tel Aviv: Histadrut, 1934) p. 174.
98. Ludwig Lewisohn, *op. cit.,* p. 307.
99. *Ibid.,* p. 11.
100. *Ibid.,* p. 345.

101. Emanuel Neumann, *The Birth of Jewish Statesmanship: the Story of Theodor Herzl's Life* (New York, Zionist Organization of America, 1949) p. 35.

102. "Priest and Prophet," *Selected Essays by Ahad Ha'am* trans. Leon Simon (Philadelphia: Jewish Publication Society of America, 1948) p. 133.

103. "Jewish and Christian Ethics," *Ahad Ha'am* trans. Leon Simon (Oxford: East and West Library, 1946) p. 128.

104. *Ibid.,* p. 130.

105. *Ibid.,* p. 73.

106. *Ibid.* p. 204.

107 *Ibid.,* p. 18.

108. F. Lachover, *History of Modern Hebrew Literature,* vol. II, in Hebrew (Tel Aviv: Dvir, 1937) p. 192.

109. Robert Gordis, *Conservative Judaism* (New York: United Synagogue of America, 1956) p. 14.

110. Jacob B. Agus, *Guideposts in Modern Judaism* (New York: Bloch Publishing Co., 1954) p. 99.

111. Hillel Bavli, "The Modern Renaissance of Hebrew Literature," *The Jews,* ed. Finkelstein, vol. II (Philadelphia: Jewish Publication Society, 1949) p. 579.

112. Leon Simon, *Ahad Ha'am A Biography* (Philadelphia: Jewish Publication Society, 1960) p. 315.

113. Cf. Yehezkel Kaufmann, *op. cit.,* vol. I, p. 190-199. For a succinct refutation in English of Ahad Ha'am's view of the "national will to live" see Jacob B. Agus, *op. cit.,* p. 145-148.

114. Leon Simon, *op. cit.,* p. 327.

115. Simon Halkin, *Modern Hebrew Literature, op. cit.,* p. 91.

116. Micha Joseph Berdichevsky, *Collected Essays,* in Hebrew (Tel Aviv: Am Oved, 1952) p. 35.

117. *Ibid.,* p. 36.

118. *Ibid.,* p. 34.

119. *Ibid.,* p. 38.

120. Berdichevsky, translated in Simon Halkin, *op. cit.,* p. 94.

121. Micha Joseph Berdichevsky, *op. cit.,* p. 40.

122. Joseph Heller, *The Zionist Idea* (New York: Schocken Books, 1949) p. 198.
123. Micha Joseph Berdichevsky, *op. cit.,* p. 375.
124. Berdichevsky, quoted in Simon Halkin, *op. cit.,* p. 92.
125. Micha Joseph Berdichevsky, *op. cit.,* p. 382.
126. *Ibid.,* p. 36.
127. *Ibid.*
128. *Ibid.,* p. 38.
129. *Ibid.,* p. 43.
130. Simon Halkin, *op. cit.,* p. 91.
131. M. Glikson, *Works,* Vol II, in Hebrew (Tel Aviv: Dvir, 1941). p. 270.
132. He delivered a paper entitled "Science and Ethics: the Contribution of Greece, India and Israel," March 9, 1960. Incidentally, Berdichevsky used the pen-name Bin Gurion.
133. Cf. B. Kurzweil, "The Young Hebrews," *Jewish Spectator* (Sept., 1953).
134. Reb Binyamin, *From Zaborov to Kinneret,* in Hebrew (Tel Aviv: Association of Hebrew Writers, 1950) p. 209, 210.
135. Y. CH. Brenner, *Collection of Stories,* in Hebrew (Tel Aviv: Israel Matz Fund, n.d.) Introduction, p. xi.
136. *Ibid.*
137. Y. CH. Brenner, "From Here and There," *Works,* vol. I, in Hebrew (Tel Aviv: Ann Oved, 1946) p. 215.
138. *Ibid.,* p. 186.
139. *Ibid.,* p. 261.
140. *Ibid.*
141. *Ibid.,* p. 274.
142. A. Orinovsky, *History of Modern Hebrew Literature, op. cit.,* p. 435.
143. Y. CH. Brenner, "Around the Point," *Works op. cit.,* p. 115.
144. Y. CH. Brenner, "Bereavement and Failure," *Works* Vol. II. *op. cit.,* p. 290.
145. I. Rabinowitz, *Temperament and Creativity,* in Hebrew (Tel Aviv: Bialik Institute, 1951) p. 249.
146. A. Orinovsky, *op. cit.,* p. 436.

147. Y. CH. Brenner, *Works,* vol. VII, in Hebrew p. 185.
148. *Ibid.,* p. 109.
149. Cited in A. Orinovsky, *op. cit.,* p. 434.
150. David Shimoni, *Chapters of Reminiscences,* in Hebrew (Tel Aviv: Dvir, 1953) p. 245.
151. Berl Katznelson, *Writings,* in Hebrew (Tel Aviv: Hapoel Hatzair, n.d.) vol. I, p. 285.
152. Reuben Wallenrod, *The Literature of Modern Israel* (New York: Abelard-Schuman, 1956) p. 92.
153. A. D. Gordon, *Selected Essays,* trans. Frances Burnce (New York: League for Labor Palestine, 1938) p. 60.
154. Moshe Smilansky, "Aaron David Gordon," *Sound the Great Trumpet,* ed. M. Z. Frank (New York: Whittier Books, 1955) p. 81.
155. A. D. Gordon, *Selected Essays, op. cit.,* p. 71, 72.
156. Shalom Speigel, *Hebrew Reborn op. cit.,* p. 410, 411.
157. A. D. Gordon, *Selected Essays, op. cit.,* p. 250, 251.
158. *Ibid.,* p. 2.
159. *Ibid.,* p. 111.
160. *Ibid.,* p. 109.
161. A. D. Gordon, *The Writings of A. D. Gordon,* in Hebrew, (Tel Aviv: Hapoel Hatzair, 1928) vol. I, p. 95.
162. *Ibid.,* p. 97.
163. A. D. Gordon, *Selected Essays,* op. cit., p. 41.
164. *Ibid.,* p. 247.
165. *Ibid.,* p. 179.
166. *Ibid.,* p. 216.
167. A. D. Gordon, *Nation and Labor,* in Hebrew (Jerusalem: Histadrut Tzionit, 1952) p. 497.
168. A. D. Gordon, *Selected Essays, op. cit.,* p. 181.
169. The title of one of Max Nordau's books.
170. A. D. Gordon, *Selected Essays, op. cit.,* p. 78.
171. Lewis Mumford's characterization in *The Condition of Man.*
172. F. Lachover, *Poetry and Thought,* in Hebrew (Tel Aviv: Dvir, 1953) p. 151.
173. A. D. Gordon, *Selected Essays, op. cit.,* p. 4.
174. *Ibid.,* p. 14.

175. Shalom Wurm, *The Kvutza* (New York: Habonim, 1942) p. 23.
176. *Ibid.*, p. 24.
177. A. D. Gordon, *The Writings of A. D. Gordon, op. cit.*, p. 255.
178. A. D. Gordon, *Selected Essays, op. cit.*, p. 48.
179. A. D. Gordon, *Nation and Labor, op. cit.*, p. 366.
180. A. D. Gordon, *The Writings of A. D. Gordon, op. cit.*, p. 250.
181. *Ibid.*, p. 249, 250.
182. A. D. Gordon, *Selected Essays, op. cit.*, p. 129.
183. *Ibid.*, p. 87.
184. A. D. Gordon, *Nation and Labor, op. cit.*, p. 367.
185. A. D. Gordon, *Selected Essays, op. cit.*, p. 39.
186. *Ibid.*, p. 13.
187. *Ibid.*, p. 373, 374.
188. *Ibid.*, p. 95.
189. A. D. Gordon, *Nation and Labor, op. cit.*, p. 584.
190. Nachman Syrkin, "The Socialist Jewish State," in *Nachman Syrkin: Socialist Zionist,* by Marie Syrkin (New York: Herzl Press, 1961) p. 271.
191. *Ibid.*, p. 268.
192. *Ibid.*, p. 274.
193. *Ibid.*, p. 282.
194. Nachman Syrkin, *Essays on Socialist Zionism* (New York: Young Poalei Zion Alliance of America, 1935) p. 28.
195. *Nachman Syrkin: Socialist Zionist, op. cit.*, p. 278.
196. Nachman Syrkin, *Writings,* vol. I, in Hebrew (Ein Harod: Hakibbutz Hameuchad, n.d.) p. 246.
197. *Ibid.*
198. Nachman Syrkin, *Essays on Socialist Zionism, op. cit.*, p. 37.
199. *Ibid.*, p. 41.
200. *Ibid.*
201. *Ibid.*, p. 53.
202. N. Syrkin, *Selected Writings,* in Yiddish (New York: Poale Zion, 1925) p. 37.
203. *Ibid.*, p. 271.

204. Marie Syrkin, *Nachman Syrkin: Socialist Zionist, op. cit.,* p. 228.

205. Ber Borochov, *Language Research and Literary History,* in Yiddish (Israel: I. L. Peretz Publishing House, 1966).

206. Ber Borochov, *Nationalism and the Class Struggle: A Marxian Approach to the Jewish Problem* (New York: Poale Zion, 1937) p. 137.

207. *Ibid.,* p. 144.

208. *Ibid.,* p. 140.

209. D. B. Borochov, *Labor Zionist Writings,* in Yiddish (New York: Poale Zion, 1920) I, p. 67.

210. B. Borochov, *Selected Writings,* in Hebrew (Tel Aviv; Am Oved, 1944) I, p. 13.

211. Ber Borochov, *Nationalism and the Class Struggle, op. cit.,* p. 191.

212. B. Borochov, *Selected Writings, op. cit.,* I, p. 140.

213. D. B. Borochov, *Labor Zionist Writings, op. cit.,* p. 289.

214. Ber Borochov, *Nationalism and the Class Struggle, op. cit.,* p. 74.

215. D. B. Borochov, *Labor Zionist Writtings, op. cit.,* p. 320.

216. Ber Borochov, *Nationalism and the Class Struggle, op. cit.,* p. 83.

217. Ber Borochov, *Selected Writings, op. cit.,* p. 2.

218. *Ibid.,* p. 86.

219. *Ibid.,* p. 146.

220. Ber Borochov, *Nationalism and the Class Struggle, op. cit.,* p. 126.

221. B. Borochov, *Selected Writings,* in Yiddish (New York: Jewish National Workers Alliance, 1928) II, p. 286.

222. *Borochov Anthology,* in Hebrew (Tel Aviv: Poale Zion, 1937) p. 46.

223. B. Borochov, *Selected Writings,* in Yiddish, *op. cit.,* II, p. 262.

224. J. L. Fishman, (ed.), *In Memoriam,* in Hebrew (Jerusalem: Mossad Horav Kuk (1937-38) p. 63.

225. *Ibid.,* p. 91.
226. *Ibid.,* p. 93.
227. *Ibid.,* p. 62.
228. *Ibid.,* p. 90.
229. *Ibid.,* p. 63.
230. Abraham Isaac Kuk, *Vision of Redemption,* in Hebrew (Jerusalem: Assoc. for Pub. Works of Chief Rabbi Kuk, 1941) p. 65.
231. Abraham Isaac Kuk, *Epistles of RAIH,* in Hebrew, (Jerusalem: Mossad Horav Kuk, 1961) p. 280.
232. Abraham Bick (ed.), Kuk in *Exponents and Philosophy of Religious Zionism.* (New York: Hashomer Hadati of North America, 1942) p. 39.
233. Abraham Isaac Kuk, *Epistles of RAIH, op. cit.,* p. 38.
234. Abraham Isaac Kuk, *Vision of Redemption, op. cit.,* p. 4.
235. Abraham Isaac Kuk, *Epistles of RAIH, op. cit.,* p. 5.
236. Abraham Isaac Kuk in Bick, *op. cit.,* p. 40.
237. Jacob B. Agus, *Banner of Jerusalem.* (New York: Bloch, 1946) p. 240.
238. Clearmont-Tannerre at the National Assembly, 1789.
239. Theodor Herzl in *Old-New Land, op. cit.*
240. Berl Katznelson, *Davar* (daily) in Hebrew, Tel Aviv, Nov. 3, 1941.
241. Arnold J. Toynbee, *A Study of History,* abridgement of volumes VII-X (New York: Oxford University Press, 1957) p. 178.
242. Isaiah 49:6.
243. Salo W. Baron, in *Great Ages and Ideas of the Jewish People,* Leo W. Schwartz, ed., (New York: Random House, 1956) p. 434.

Selected Bibliography

A. PRIMARY SOURCES AVAILABLE IN ENGLISH*

Ahad Ha-Am. Simon, Leon (ed.) Translated from the Hebrew, Essays, letters, memoirs, Oxford: East and West Library, 1946.

——— *Nationalism and the Jewish Ethic,* basic writings, New York: Herzl Press, 1962.

——— *Selected Essays.* Philadelphia: J.P.S., 1948.

——— (Asher Ginzberg) *The Persistence of Judaism.* Essays edited by Hans Kohn. New York: Schocken, 1962.

Baratz, Joseph. *A Village by the Jordan: The Story of Degania.* New York: Sharon, 1957.

Ben-Gurion, David. *Israel: Years of Challenge.* New York, Holt, Rinehart and Winston, 1963.

Bick, Abraham (ed.) *Exponents and Philosophy of Religious Zionism,* an anthology; selections from the writings of the fathers of religious Zionism with brief biographical sketches and characterizations. Brooklyn: Hashomer Hadati of North America, 1942.

* Does not include bibliographical references in other languages listed in the notes.

Borochov, Ber. *Nationalism and the Class Struggle: A Marxian Approach to the Jewish Problem.* New York: Poale Zion, 1937.

Brandeis, Louis D. *Brandeis on Zionism.* Washington: Zionist Organization of America, 1942.

Buber, Martin. *Israel and Palestine.* New York: Farrar, Straus and Young, 1952.

Dinur, Ben Zion. *Israel and the Diaspora.* Philadelphia: JPS, 1965.

Gordon, A. D. *Selected Essays.* Translated by Frances Burnce. New York: League for Labor Palestine, 1938.

Hertzberg, Arthur (ed.) *The Zionist Idea; a Historical Analysis and Reader.* New York: Harper Torchbooks, 1960.

Herzl, Theodor. *The Jewish State.* New York: American Zionist Emergency Council, 1946.

———*Old-New Land.* Translated by L. Levensohn. New York: Bloch Publishing Company, 1941.

——— *Complete Diaries.* Edited by R. Patai. New York: Herzl Press, 1960.

Hess, Moses. *Rome and Jerusalem.* Translated by Meyer Waxman. New York: Bloch Publishing Company, 1945.

Lowenthal, Marvin. *The Diaries of Theodor Herzl.* New York: Dial, 1956.

Meir, Golda. *This is our Strength.* New York: Macmillan, 1962.

Nordau, Max. *Max Nordau to His people. A summons and a challenge.* New York: Scopus, 1941.

Pinsker, Leo. *Auto-Emancipation.* Translated by C. S. Blondheim. New York: Zionist Organization of America, 1948.

——— *Road to Freedom.* New York: Scopus, 1944.

Syrkin, Nachman. *Essays on Socialist Zionism.* New York: Young Poalei Zion Alliance of America, 1935.

Weizmann, Chaim. *Trial and Error: The Autobiography of Chaim Weizmann, First President of Israel.* New York: Harper and Row, 1949.

B. BIOGRAPHY

Agus, Jacob B. *Banner of Jerusalem: The Life, Times and Thought of Abraham Isaac Kuk, Late Chief Rabbi of Palestine.* New York: Bloch Publishing Company, 1946.

Bein, A. *Theodor Herzl: A Biography.* Philadelphia: Jewish Publication Society, 1951.

Ben Horin, Meir. *Max Nordau.* New York: Herzl, 1956.

Cohen, Israel. *Theodor Herzl: Founder of Political Zionism.* New York: Herzl, 1959.

Dayan, Samuel. *Pioneers in Israel.* New York: World, 1961.

Fineman, Irving. *Woman of Valor: The Life of Henrietta Szold.* New York: Simon and Schuster, 1961.

Freundlich, Charles H. *Peretz Smolenskin: His life and thought. A study of the renascence of Jewish nationalism.* New York: Bloch Publishing Co., 1965.

Lewisohn, Ludwig. (ed.) *Theodor Herzl: A Portrait for This Age.* Cleveland: World Publishing Company, 1955.

Lipsky, Louis. *A Gallery of Zionist Profiles.* New York: Farrar, Straus and Cudahy, 1956.

Rose, Herbert H. *The Life and Thought of A. D. Gordon: Pioneer, Philosopher and Prophet of Modern Israel.* New York: Bloch, 1964.

Rosenberger, Edwin. *Herzl As I Remember Him.* New York: Herzl, 1959.

Rosensaft, Menachem Z. *Moshe Sharett: Statesman of Israel.* New York: Shengold, 1968.

Samuel, Maurice. (ed.) *Forward From Exile.* Philadelphia: JPS, 1967.

St. John, Robert. *Ben-Gurion.* New York: Doubleday, 1959.

——— *They Came from Everywhere: Twelve Who Helped Mold Modern Israel.* New York: Coward McCann, 1962.

——— *Tongue of the Prophets: The Life Story of Eliezer Ben-Yehuda.* New York: Doubleday, 1952.

Schulman, Mary. *Moses Hess: Prophet of Zionism.* New York: Yoseloff, 1963.

Simon, Sir Leon. *Ahad Ha-Am, Asher Ginzberg: A Biography.* Philadelphia: Jewish Publication Society, 1960.

Spiegel, Shalom. *Hebrew Reborn.* New York: Macmillan Company, 1930.

Sykes, Christopher (Hugh). *Orde Wingate.* London: Collins, 1959.

Syrkin, Marie. *Golda Meir: The Woman With A Cause.* New York: Putnam, 1963.

——— *Nachman Syrkin: Socialist Zionist.* New York: Herzl and Sharon, 1961.

Wise, Stephen S. *Challenging Years.* New York: Putnam, 1949.

C. HISTORY, PHILOSOPHY, SOCIOLOGY, AND CULTURE

Bar-David, M. L. *My Promised Land.* New York: Putnam, 1953.

Baratz, Gideon and Others. *A New Way of Life: The Collective Settlement of Israel.* London: Shindler and Golomb, with the Anglo-Israel Association, 1949.

Barer, Shlomo. *The Magic Carpet.* New York: Harper, 1952.

Begin, Menahem. *The Revolt. Story of the Irgun.* New York: Schuman, 1951.

Ben-Gurion, David. (ed.) *The Jews in their Land.* Garden City, New York: Doubleday, 1966.

Bein, Alexander. *The Return to the Soil: A History of Jewish Settlement in Israel.* Jerusalem: Youth and Hechalutz Department of the Zionist Organization, 1952.

Ben-Yosef, Avraham C. *The Purest Democracy in the World.* New York: Herzl and Yoseloff, 1963.

Bentwich, Norman. *Israel Resurgent.* New York: Praeger, 1960.

Bergman, Samuel Hugo. *Faith and Reason.* New York: Schocken, 1966.

Bermant, Chaim. *Israel.* Washington: Current Affairs, 1968.

Bilby, Kenneth W. *New Star in the Near East.* New York: Doubleday, 1951.

Bondy, Ruth, Ohad Zemora and Raphael Bashan (eds.) *Mission Survival.* New York: Sabra, 1968.

Cohen, Israel. *The Zionist Movement.* Edited by Bernard G. Richards. New York: Zionist Organization of America, 1946.

Crossman, Richard H. S. *A Nation Reborn.* New York: Atheneum, 1960.

Crum, Bartley C. *Behind the Silken Curtain: A Personal Account of Anglo-American Diplomacy in Palestine and the Middle East.* New York: Simon and Schuster, 1947.

Davis, Moshe. (ed.) *Israel: It's Role in Civilization.* New York: Seminary Israel Institute of the Jewish Theological Seminary of America, distributed by Harper, 1956.

Dayan, Moshe. *Diary of the Sinai Campaign.* New York: Harper and Row, 1966.

Dunner, Joseph. *Democratic Bulwark in the Middle East.* Grinnell, Iowa: Grinnell College, 1953.

——— *Republic of Israel: Its History and Its Promise.* New York: McGraw, 1950.

Eban, Abba Solomon. *Voice of Israel.* New York: Horizon Press, 1957.

Eisenstadt, Samuel N. *The Absorption of Immigrants.* Glencoe, Illinois: Free Press, 1955.

——— *Israeli Society.* New York: Praeger, 1967.

Fishman, Aryeh (ed.) *The Religious Kibbutz Movement.* Jerusalem: 1957.

Frank, M. Z. *Sound the Great Trumpet.* New York: Whittier Books, 1955.

Gamzey, Robert. *Miracle of Israel.* New York: Herzl, 1965.

Garcia, Granados. *The Birth of Israel; The Drama as I Saw It.* New York: Alfred A. Knopf, 1948.

Goldberg, Israel. *Fulfillment: The Epic Story of Zionism.* By Rufus Learsi (pseud.). Cleveland: World Publishing Company, 1951.

Halkin, Simon. *Modern Hebrew Literature: Trends and Values.* New York: Schocken Books, 1950.

Halperin, Haim. *Changing Patterns in Israel Agriculture.* London: Routledge and Kegan Paul, 1957.

Halpern, Ben. *The Idea of the Jewish State.* Cambridge, Mass: Harvard University, 1961.

Heller, Joseph. *The Zionist Idea.* New York: Schocken Books, 1949.

Horowitz, David. *State in the Making.* Translated by Julian Meltzer. New York: Knopf, 1953.

——— *The Economics of Israel.* Oxford: Pergamon Press, 1967.

Hyamson, Albert M. *Palestine Under the Mandate: 1920-1948.* London: Methuen, 1950.

Jabotinsky, Vladimir. *The Story of the Jewish Legion.* New York: Bernard Ackerman, 1945.

Janowsky, Oscar. *Foundations of Israel: Emergence of a Welfare State.* Princeton: Van Nostrand, 1959.

Joseph, Bernard. *British Rule in Palestine.* Washington: Public Affairs Press, 1948.

Kallen, Horace M. *Utopians at Bay.* New York: Herzl, 1958.

Kanovsky, Eliyaho. *The Economy of the Israeli Kubbutz.* Cambridge, Mass.: Harvard University, 1966.

Kimche, Jon and David. *Both Sides of the Hill.* London: Secker and Warburg, 1960.

Kling, Simcha. *Nachum Sokolow: Servant of His People.* New York: Herzl, 1960.

Laufer, Leopold. *Israel and the Developing Countries: New Approaches to Cooperation.* New York: Twentieth Century Fund, 1967.

Litvinoff, Barnet. *To the House of Their Fathers; A History of Zionism.* New York: Oxford University Press, 1949.

MacDonald, James G. *My Mission in Israel. 1948-51.* New York: Simon and Schuster, 1951.

Matras, Judah. *Social Change in Israel.* Chicago: Aldine, 1965.

Mead, Margaret. *Israel and the Problems of Identity.* New York: Herzl, 1958.

Meeker, Oden. *Israel Reborn.* New York: Scribner, 1964.

Miller, Irving. *Israel, The Eternal Ideal.* New York: Farrar, Strauss and Cudahy, 1955.

Parzen, Herbert. *A Short History of Zionism.* New York: Herzl Press, 1962.

Patai, Raphael. *Israel Between East and West: A Study in Human Relations.* Philadelphia: Jewish Publication Society, 1953.

Pearlman, Moshe. *Army of Israel.* New York: Philosophical Library, 1950.

——— *Ben-Gurion Looks Back.* New York: Simon and Schuster, 1965.

Prittie, Terrence. *Israel: Miracle in the Desert.* New York: Praeger, 1967.

Sachar, Howard. *From Ends of the Earth, the people of Israel.* Cleveland: World Publishing Co., 1964.

Safran, Nadav. *Israel Today: A Profile.* New York: Foreign Policy Association, 1965.

St. John, Robert. *Shalom Means Peace.* Garden City, N.Y.: Doubleday, 1949.

Samuel, Maurice. *Harvest in the Desert.* Philadelphia: Jewish Publication Society, 1944.

——— *Level Sunlight.* New York: Alfred A. Knopf, 1953.

——— *What Happened in Palestine.* Boston: Stratford Company, 1931.

Schwartz, I. Z. *Israel's War of Liberation.* Translated by Itzchak Ivry. Jerusalem: Mass, 1951.

Singer, Howard. *Bring Forth the Mighty Men: On Violence and the Jewish character.* New York: Funk & Wagnalls, 1969.

Spiro, Melford E. *Kibbutz: Venture in Utopia.* Cambridge: Harvard University Press, 1956.

Stock, Ernest. *From Conflict to Understanding. Relations Between Jews and Arabs in Israel since 1948.* New York: Institute of Human Relations Press. American Jewish Committee, 1968.

Tauber, Esther. *Molding Society to Man.* New York: Bloch Publishing Company, 1955.

Viteles Harry. *A History of the Co-operative Movement in Israel.* London: Valentine, 1967-8.

Voss, Carl Hermann. *Palestine Problem Today: Israel and its Neighbors.* Boston: Beacon, 1954.

Wallenrod, Reuben. *The Literature of Modern Israel.* New York: Abelard-Schuman, 1957.

Weingarten, Murray. *Life in a Kibbutz.* Jerusalem: Zionist Organization, Youth and Hechaulutz Department, 1959.

Weingrod, Alex. *Israel.* New York: Praeger, 1965.

Weisbord, Robert G. *African Zion.* Philadelphia: Jewish Publication Society of America, 1968.

Wurm, Shalom. *The Kvutza.* New York: Habonim, 1942.

D. EDUCATION

Avidor, M. *Education in Israel.* Jerusalem: Youth and Hechalutz Department of the Zionist Organization, 1957.

Bentwich, Joseph. *Education in Israel.* Philadelphia: J.P.S., 1965.

Braham, Randolph. *Israel: A Modern Education System. A Report emphasizing secondary and teacher education.* Washington: United States Department of Health, Education and Welfare, 1966.

Nardi, Noah. *Education in Palestine.* New York: Zionist Organization of America, 1945.

E. DOCUMENTARY

The Arab War Against Israel. Jerusalem: Ministry for Foreign Affairs, 1967.

Book of Documents Submitted to the General Assembly of the United Nations. The Jewish Agency for Palestine. New York: May, 1947.

Eight Years of Israel Independence. New York: Israel Office of Information, 1956.

Facts About Israel. Annual. Jerusalem: Ministry of Foreign Affairs, 1959.

Israel. Annual. New York: Israel Office of Information 1952-1958.

Israel: Government Year Book 1950. Annual. Jerusalem: Government Printer, 1950.

Israel: Laws of State 1949. Annual. Jerusalem: Government Printer, 1949.

Israel Must be Annihilated. Tel Aviv: Zahal Information Office, 1967.

Index